Routledge Revivals

Terrorism and Communism

First published in English in 1920, this is a reissue of Karl Kautsky's seminal work dealing with the origins and history of the forces at work in revolutionary epochs, which offers path breaking insights into the development of civilisation.

The opening chapters, dealing with eighteenth century France, are of special interest to the student of the French revolution. The section devoted to the Commune of Paris offers a stimulating and provocative description of this famous government of the working class.

The reissue of this controversial and extraordinary work will be welcomed by all those interested in the history of Communism in particular and the theory and history of revolution in general.

Terrorism and Communism

A Contribution to the Natural History of
Revolution

Karl Kautsky

Translated by
W. H. Kerridge

Routledge
Taylor & Francis Group
LONDON AND NEW YORK

First published in 1920
by George Allen & Unwin

This edition first published in 2011 by Routledge
4 Park Square, Milton Park, Abingdon, Oxon, OX14 4RN

Simultaneously published in the USA and Canada
by Routledge
605 Third Avenue, New York, NY 10017

Routledge is an imprint of the Taylor & Francis Group, an informa business

Publisher's Note
The publisher has gone to great lengths to ensure the quality of this
reprint but points out that some imperfections in the original copies may
be apparent.

Disclaimer
The publisher has made every effort to trace copyright holders and
welcomes correspondence from those they have been unable to contact.

A Library of Congress record exists under LC Control Number: 21006887

ISBN 13: 978-0-415-68519-1 (hbk)
ISBN 13: 978-0-203-80232-8 (ebk)
ISBN 13: 978-0-415-68575-7 (pbk)

TERRORISM AND COMMUNISM

A CONTRIBUTION *to the* NATURAL
HISTORY OF REVOLUTION

BY

KARL KAUTSKY

TRANSLATED BY W. H. KERRIDGE

THE NATIONAL LABOUR PRESS LTD.
LONDON : 8 & 9, JOHNSON'S COURT, E.C.4.
MANCHESTER : 30, BLACKFRIARS STREET.

First published in 1920.

PREFACE.

The following work was begun about a year ago, but was dropped as the result of the Revolution of November 9; for the Revolution brought me other obligations than merely theoretical and historical research. It was only after several months that I could return to the work in order, with occasional interruptions, to bring this book to a close.

The course of recent events did not minister to the uniformity of this work. It was rendered more difficult by the fact that, as time went on, the examination of this subject shifted itself to some extent. My starting point represented the central problem of modern Socialism, the attitude of Social Democracy to Bolshevik methods. But since Bolshevism had, of its own accord, referred to the Paris Commune of 1871 as being to some extent its precursor and its prototype, and as having received the sanction of Marx himself, and since the Commune is little known and understood by the present generation, I undertook to draw a parallel between the Commune and the Soviet Republic.

In order to make the Commune comprehensible I had to refer to the Paris Commune, and afterwards to the French Revolution and its Reign of Terror. This gave me fresh means for another parallel to the Soviet Republic; hence an examination of the Commune led to an examination of Terrorism, its origin and its consequences.

Thus there are two lines of thought which become merged in this book, the one occasionally leading away from the other. At first I felt this to be rather disturbing, and even considered whether it would not be better to divide the work into two separate sections, the one representing the exposition of the Commune, the other a discussion of Terrorism. However, in regard to my starting point, the Soviet Republic is in such very close connection with these two events in history, that it seemed to me impossible to treat them separately. I hope therefore that, in spite of the difficulties inherent in the dual nature of this book, I shall have succeeded in preserving uniformity in the structure of the thoughts contained therein.

However academic the reader may think many of my illustrations and expositions, they are all of the highest practical importance, especially at such a wildly fermented time as the present. This does not mean to say that I have adapted, as it were, the truth to the needs of the moment. Instead I have always sought, even in those sections where I was referring to a period long past, to treat only of that side of the subject which seemed calculated to throw light upon the chaos that surrounds us.

If we regard only this chaos as it exists in Russia and Germany at the present moment, our prospects at the moment and our future must be very far from cheering. We see a world sinking under economic ruin and fratricidal murder. In both countries we find Socialists under the Governments acting against other Socialists, with similar cruelty to that practised more than half a century ago by the Versailles butchers of the Commune —cruelty which has earned the most laudable indignation of the whole International Proletariat ever since.

Nevertheless, the outlook becomes brighter so soon as we consider the International. The workers of West Europe have arisen. It rests with them to accomplish actual results, only with more worthy methods than those practised up to the present in the East.

Hence it is necessary that they should learn from us, and that they should learn to recognise the different methods of struggle, as well as of construction, by their results. It is not so much a blind adulation of the methods of the Revolution hitherto prevailing, but the strictest criticism which is necessary, and especially necessary just at present, when the Revolution and the Socialist Parties are passing through a most difficult crisis, in which different methods are struggling to gain the ascendancy.

The success of the Revolution will depend not a little on whether or not it discovers the right methods of carrying the revolutionary message to the Proletariat. To examine methods is at the present moment our highest duty. To help with this examination and thus to further the Revolution is the object of this present work.

KARL KAUTSKY.

Charlottenburg, June, 1919.

CONTENTS.

Terrorism and Communism.

CHAPTER I

REVOLUTION AND TERROR.

UP to the outbreak of war, the idea was current in the widest circles of social democracy that the time for revolutions, not only for West Europe, but also for Germany and Austria, was long since past. Whoever thought differently was scoffed at as a revolutionary romancer.

Now we have the Revolution with us, and it is taking on forms of barbarity, which even the most fantastic of revolutionary romancers could scarce have expected.

The abolition of the death penalty was for every social democrat a perfectly obvious claim. The Revolution, however, has brought with it the most bloody terrorism practised by Socialist Governments. The Bolsheviks in Russia started this, and were in consequence condemned in the most bitter terms by all who did not accept the Bolshevik standpoint. Among them are the German Majority Socialists. But these latter hardly felt their own power threatened before they resorted to the same means practised by the Regiment of Terror, which have characterised the Revolution in the East. Noske has boldly followed in Trotsky's footsteps; certainly with this difference, that he himself does not regard his dictatorship as the dictatorship of the proletariat. But both justify their slaughter on the grounds of the rights of the Revolution.

B

It is, in fact, a widely spread idea that Terrorism belongs to the very essence of revolution, and that whoever wants a revolution must somehow come to some sort of terms with Terrorism. As proof of this assertion, over and over again the great French Revolution has been cited. It is regarded as the Revolution *par excellence*.

An examination of Terrorism, of its conditions and consequences, can best proceed from a description of the Regiment of Terror instituted by the Sans-culotists. With this we will begin. This will take us back some considerable distance from contemporary events, but these we shall better understand after an examination of the past. It is striking to find how many resemblances there are between the great French Revolution and the revolutions of the present time, especially the Russian.

Yet the revolutions of our times differ in many essential points from the revolution of the 18th century. This is shown at once by a comparison of our proletariat, our industry and commerce, with the corresponding phenomena of that period.

CHAPTER II.

PARIS.

THE present German Revolution has no centre, whereas the French Revolution was controlled from Paris. That Revolution, as well as the Regiment of Terror that operated within it, are quite incapable of comprehension, without a consideration of the economic and political importance which Paris had acquired for France as a whole. No town in the 18th, or indeed the 19th century has exercised such power as did Paris at that period. This was due to the importance which the royal residence as being the central Government possesses in a modern bureaucratic centralised State, so long as economic decentralisation, which modern industrial capitalism and the development of means of transport bring in its train, has not set in.

In a feudal State the powers of its central body, of its monarch, are in reality very few. Its functions do not extend very far, nor is the corresponding government apparatus at all large. This apparatus can be very easily transferred from one city or estate to another. The monarch is all the more often compelled to resort to this measure, so long as the system of transport remains in an undeveloped state, and so long as the separate localities do not suffice to maintain him and his retainers. Hence he has more urgent cause to visit personally the different regions of his domain, since this is the only means whereby he may count on preserving their fealty and obedience. In those early times, therefore, it was the chief business of the monarch to wander from place to place like a nomad, seeking out one rich pasturage after the other, forsaking it as soon as he had exhausted its possibilities.

3

In process of time, however, the government apparatus undergoes development, especially as a result of the increase in production, which the money system makes possible, and which exacts tribute in payment of easily transportable coin, instead of cumbrous natural products. In proportion to the increase of tribute, the power of the monarch increases also, likewise the government apparatus in the form of a bureaucracy and a standing army. Wandering from place to place thus becomes impossible. Monarch and government must be established in some fixed place. In former days single large towns were the central points of commerce, being situate in the centre of the kingdom and wealthier than the smaller provincial towns. Thus they eventually became capitals, which the monarch chose as his place of residence, and henceforward one special city was chosen for the permanent abode of both government and monarch. Here there were soon collected together all who had to do with the government, and it was to this quarter that the taxes of the whole kingdom came, only a part of which ever found its way back. It was here that tradesmen in the service of court and government settled down, as well as financiers, who came as bankers to do business with the State.

At the same time, the power of the monarch exceeded that of the nobility, whose independence was soon broken. The monarch would not tolerate the actions of the great nobleman who would settle down on his own estates, far from the king's residence. He was to remain at the court, under his personal supervision, in exclusive service on the monarch, which was service in very truth, vain and profitless. His independent functions in the administration of the public services were taken from him, and given to bureaucrats and officials whom the monarch appointed and paid. The courtiers were gradually reduced to being mere drones, whose one duty in life it was to sit at the royal court and dissipate the revenue obtained from their own estates. What they, therefore, in early days consumed in their own castles and fortresses, together with their retainers, soon flowed into the court town and increased its wealth. There they built new palaces alongside of the king's; they squandered their riches in riotous living, since they were deprived of all serious office. And the capitalist "parvenus," who came to the fore with them, tried to imitate them.

Thus the royal residences, as distinct from the country places and the "provincial towns," became not merely the centre of the wealth of the whole country, but the centre also of a life of pleasure. This exercised a strong hold over those in the country and, indeed, many outside, who had the means to live a life of enjoyment, or who had the inclination and the capacity for acting as ministrants of joy to the pleasure-seekers, whom they succeeded in fleecing.

But more serious-minded people were attracted to the residence towns. Whereas the nobles who lived on their solitary estates had nothing for pastime except to eat and drink, hunt and make merry with the girls of the neighbourhood, the town introduced finer manners and pleasures. The nobility began to evince an interest in the arts, and the patronising of science soon became the "fashion." Thus artists and intellectual men soon gathered to the royal residence, where they hoped more speedily to gain advancement. The more the bourgeoisie increased in number in the residential towns, the more the artists and writers flocked to the place, hoping there, alongside of the nobility, to find some foothold and a market for their wares. Thus it is clear that numbers of industrial people and dealers were drawn to the place, in order to meet the requirements and needs of all these elements. Nowhere was there such prospect of making one's fortune as in the royal residence towns

Thither flocked all who had intelligence, self-confidence, and energy.

Yet it was not everyone who accomplished his object. There were numerous cases of failures, who formed another characteristic of the capital. They were the crowds of the riff-raff proletariat, who sought to better themselves in the capital, because it was there that they could best hide themselves and await the turns of fortune, which they could soon put to advantage. They were men such as Riccaut de la Martinière. Not only art and science, but also unbridled pleasure-seeking, along with bitterest poverty and frequent crime, became another feature of the royal capital.

Corresponding to the peculiar social position was a peculiarity of mental attitude which animated the population. But it was not the same in every royal residence. Quantity often gave place to quality.

In a small state, or in a community that was economically in a backward condition, the residential town was small, so that many of the characteristics mentioned above were lacking. In such a town the most prominent feature was the dependence of the inhabitants on the court, and this dependence was not only economical and political, but spiritual as well. The mentality of the courtier became coarser, rougher, and more naïve, and was reflected in the provincial population, who derived their light from the capital.

This was the origin of the strongly monarchic and servile mentality of the German people and its attendant "provincialism." It was a mentality which, at the time of the rise of the bourgeois democracy, brought its pioneers to the forefront. It caused the desperate Börne to declare : " Other peoples are servants. The Germans are those who are served "— a thought more cynically expressed by Heine : " Germany, the pious children's nursery, is not a Roman den of murderers."

But mental and spiritual conditions were different in a large royal town. The larger the town, the smaller the number and influence of the people attracted to the court, as against the rest of the population, who sought to establish their fortunes there. The greater the number of the disillusioned and dissatisfied, the greater became their solidarity and their strength. This state of affairs did not encourage those people alone; it strengthened the opposition of those who, without having personal grounds for grievance, nevertheless clearly recognised the harm from which State and society were suffering. Such opposition was everywhere rife. In the smaller towns it lay dormant, in the larger towns it dared to express itself.

Among the royal residences of the continent in the 17th and 18th centuries the largest was Paris, capital of the most important State at that time in Europe. It numbered, at the end of the 18th century, about 600,000 inhabitants. Weimar, the royal residence and the spiritual centre of Germany, numbered about 10,000.

The inhabitants of Paris early showed their rebellious spirit. Thus arose the agitation of the Frondes in 1648, which had as its origin the conflict between the government and the Paris Parliament, which was the supreme tribunal. Barricades were erected, until finally the King had to flee Paris. This was in 1649, the same year in which Charles First was beheaded in England. The struggle lasted until 1652, in which year the monarchy had to come to some agreement, which, however, soon led to the re-establishment of absolutism. The capital had united with the high nobility in the fight, and that formed an unequal combination. And the high nobility could carry nothing to success against the monarchy. Paris had not the same power of opposition to act against Louis that London had against Charles.

The struggle of the Frondes took place when Louis XIV. was still adolescent. The rising of the Parisians and his flight made a deep impression upon him. In order not again to experience similar humiliation, he established his residence outside Paris. Of course, he was obliged to leave the Government machinery behind; but as the settled place for his court he chose a spot that was near enough to Paris to ensure a permanent and quick means of communication with the royal residence, yet far enough distant to be protected from any street disturbances. In the year 1672 the building of his new palace, which was to cost him, or rather, his people, a million of francs, was begun in Versailles, 12 miles distant from Paris. In the coming centuries it often gave proof that it had been built in defiance of the rebels in Paris.

Although Paris often rose in determined opposition to the central power of the State, its attitude towards that power did not always give token of unified action. On the one hand, it strove for independence and detachment from the State power, and yet its wealth and power depended on the size of the empire, and on the strength of the State power in the empire. It strove for the autonomy of the community, and yet drew the greater advantage from State centralisation which, itself, by its very existence, it encouraged.

It was the prominent position of Paris over all other parts of the Empire which, in the course of that 18th century, welded together the different conquered provinces of France in such sound national unity. What otherwise could have united the Alsatians with the Bretons, or the Flemings with the Gascoigners? But they all had relations with Paris. Their finest sons were to be found there, where they merged into one single and unified nation. The contradiction occasioned by the fact that Paris formed, at one and at the same time, the strongest support of the centralising State power, as well as its most vigorous opposition, was reflected in the attitude of Paris towards the provinces. In Paris the evils and abuses from which the Empire was suffering were quickest brought to light. Paris had, more than any other place, the courage to expose and brand them. It soonest acquired the strength to attack them. Hence it became the protagonist of the whole of suffering France. The people in the provinces, through being scattered about, were backward in intelligence, and were dispirited and powerless. They saw in Paris their pioneer, their saviour, and they often followed the lead given by Paris with the utmost enthusiasm.

Yet not always. For this very Paris became large and powerful, not only because of the labours of its inhabitants, but also through the exploitation of the provinces, which resulted in the lion's share of the commodities created in the provinces flowing into Paris, where it was partly squandered and partly turned to account for the accumulation of capital, for the enrichment and strengthening of the exploiters and profiteers in the country. Hence, along with the confidence reposed in progressive Paris, there was engendered a genuine hatred of Paris as an exploiting capital; thus arose opposition between the royal residence and the provinces. According to the historical situation, sometimes the one, sometimes the other gained the upper hand.

The economical opposition was rendered more striking because of the different points of view, which arose from the differences in the social milieu. In the open country and in the provinces economic stagnation was apparent. Hence the conservatism and adherence to traditional moral views. Moreover, whosoever would not acknowledge these views had to conceal the fact; for in the narrow circles of village and small town everyone was under the control of the whole community.

Such control was entirely lacking in a very large town. There one could afford to be bold and laugh to scorn obsolete traditions. And these traditions were attacked from above as well as from below: that is to say, as much by the arrogant pleasure-seeking nobility and the capitalists as by the masses of the lower orders, who in their misery and their continuous uncertainty would not be deterred by considerations for private property, having lost their respect for family life. Between these two sections there stood large groups of intellectuals and parasites, who were often in as deep misery as the beggar proletariat, although they had access to some of the pleasurable life enjoyed by the resident nobility and the large financiers.

It was no wonder, therefore, that the modest bourgeois and the peasants were as much horrified by the crass immorality of this Babel of the Seine, as the witty Parisians were inclined to deride the barren philistinism and the narrow prejudices of the provincials.

In religious matters the same opposition arose as in the case of morals. For the peasants, in their seclusion from the world, the cleric was the only educated person who troubled about them, who established some means of communication between them and the outer world, and who supplied them with some knowledge beyond the range of the church steeple. The fact that this knowledge had long been surpassed by the rapid development of science could make no impression on the mind of the illiterate peasants in the open country. They clung to Church and religion, showing respect, however, only for the spiritual treasures of these institutions. They showed no inclination to acquire for themselves the material possessions of the Church.

For the Parisians, on the other hand, the Church property was of less importance than the influence of the Church and her conceptions of religion.

If in the Middle Ages the Church was a means for acquiring and guarding knowledge; the civil and secular knowledge, ever since the Renaissance, had long surpassed that supplied by the Church. To the people of the towns the Church appeared to be no more a means for extending knowledge, but rather for hindering it. The opposition was rendered more bitter through the attempt by the clericals to come off equal with the secularists (of whose superiority they were becoming increasingly aware), by the introduction of State measures of repression and compulsion, made in their defence. The secularists retaliated with their sharpest intellectual weapons and with crushing contempt, as well as with the most thorough methods of scientific research. They conducted the campaign against the Church with all the more zeal and interest, because by these methods, and under the conditions then prevailing, they bid fair to win over the dominant aristocrats and the bureaucrats, or at least to ensure their neutral position, provided they, in their zeal, should proceed with due caution. For the aristocrats, as well as the bureaucrats, not only despised the teachings of traditional religion; they found the Catholic Church a frequent handicap to them, because it would not unconditionally ally itself with rating State apparatus. Thus the struggle against the Church was less dangerous than the fight with absolutism; and hence the rising opposition in the State devoted its energy first to settling matters with the Church.

But even in this we find a certain divergence. The reigning bodies set themselves in opposition to the Church wherever it showed aspirations to become an independent organisation, but the Church nevertheless appeared to them to be indispensable as a means for keeping the lower orders in subjection. This divergence was noticeable even in the circles of the extreme intellectuals. Voltaire coined the phrase, " *Ecrasez l'infame* "—"Down with the infamous (Church) "—

but he discovered that religion must be preserved for the people.

A similar cleavage made its appearance in the lower ranks of the Paris populace and their leaders. Certainly they were all in opposition to the Church, and wished to have nothing to do with it. But according to the class position of the proletariat, which is always inclined to draw hard conclusions and adopt radical solutions, some of their number preached and propagated the most thorough-going atheism and materialism. Others there were who were repelled by this line of thinking, because it was the creed adopted by the aristocrats and capitalist exploiters, especially of the revolutionary period. The opposition between the believing and the atheistical Socialists was maintained in France up to well in the 19th century. Even Louis Blanc in his " History of the French Revolution " placed himself on the side of Rousseau and Robespierre, who, in opposition to the atheists, Diderot and Anarchasis Cloots, clung to their belief in God : " They realised that atheism sanctifies confusion among men because it presupposes anarchy in heaven." Louis Blanc overlooked the fact that, for the atheist, heaven exists just as little as the Lord God himself. As in the case with direct class opposition, all these differences and contradictions were bound to lead, through a gigantic upheaval like the Revolution, to the bitterest conflicts.

CHAPTER III.

Louis XIV., the same who, out of fear, had fled from Paris to Versailles, which he chose as his residence, succeeded in breaking down the last attempts of the nobility to acquire their independence. He was also strong enough in the struggles with his neighbours to extend his kingdom, and make it one of the greatest and most powerful States in Europe. But he attained this only after a series of bitter struggles, which left France thoroughly exhausted and brought her to the very brink of ruin.

His last war, the Spanish War of Succession, which lasted from 1701 till 1714, and ended unsuccessfully for France, would itself have been sufficient to cause a revolution, if a strong revolutionary class had already been in existence. The bitter feeling against the monarch was enormous. That is shown by his death in 1715.

" His burial was carried out in the simplest manner possible, in order ' to save time and money.' The people of Paris, who now believed itself freed from an intolerable yoke, followed the hearse of the great king during its passage through the streets, not only shouting out angry curses and maledictions, but actually hurling mud and stones. Round about the provinces there arose a shout of joy, mingled with curses on the deceased. Everywhere thanksgivings were held. The good fortune to be delivered from such a despot betrayed itself openly and without shame. Peace, liberty of action, lowered taxes were the benefits that the people hoped to derive from the Regent." (M. Phillippson, " The Period of Louis XIV.," p. 518.)

The people of France were doomed to bitter experiences with the followers of the " King's Son " before they were able, through the great Revolution, to take their own fortunes in their own hands.

Scarcely had the country begun to recover, to some extent, when it was plunged into new wars.   From 1733 to 1735 it was at war with Austria, for the sake of Poland and Lorraine; 1740 to 1748 it took part in the Austrian War of Succession on the side of Prussia against Maria Theresa and England; 1778 to 1783 they were able, through the great Revolution, to take their own fortunes into their own hands.

" These wars not only ruined the country; they were so miserably conducted, that they brought the French no military glory whatever." (Rossbach).

Absolutism, with the help of the rising bourgeoisie, had overthrown the feudal nobility—not, however, in order to abolish it, but rather to exercise unlimited power over it.   The monarch felt that the nobility were indispensable to him. He chose as leaders of the State policy, and of the army, members of the nobility who still showed devotion to him; but at the same time he deprived this same nobility of all independence. He degraded them until they led a parasitic life of pleasure, thus allowing them to become morally and spiritually decadent, and leading them on to economic ruin.

The more apparent the moral, intellectual and economic bankruptcy of the nobility became, the greater were the claims of that nobility on the peasantry, the more excessive their oppression and subjection, and the more did their agricultural pursuits lose in economic certainty.   At the same time, the claims of the nobles on the unhappy peasants, whom they regarded as the chief contributors to the taxes, increased enormously.   For the nobility, not content with having ruined the State through their diplomacy and military ventures, sought to compensate them-

selves for their economic decline by resorting to
plunder. In this they had the Church as well as the
monarchy to aid them, for they represented the great
landed proprietors of the State.

Over against these desperate conditions in Paris was
to be found a strong and rapidly rising bourgeoisie,
with a numerous body of intellectuals, who quickly
realised the evils affecting the State and social order,
and who branded them more unsparingly and denounced
them more destructively than any intellectuals in other
large cities in Europe could have done. And below
them was a small bourgeoisie, the most powerful and
with the greatest amount of self-assurance in Europe,
as well as a proletariat than which none was more
numerous, more concentrated, more desperate and
determined.

A fearful conflict was inevitable as soon as these
opposing forces should become arraigned against one
another. It broke out when finally the monarchy
could do no more, and at a time when financial ruin
was threatening, since no financier would advance
more credit.

The feudal councils, which had not met since 1614,
and which embodied a permanent representation of
the nobility, the clericals, the ordinary citizens, were
called upon to help, to sanction new taxes and loans,
and so help to raise the credit of bankrupt absolutism,
and infuse it with fresh life. The elections for the
individual councils were proclaimed in 1789, and the
elected were summoned to the King's palace at
Versailles.

However, with the exception of the courtiers, all
classes were too embittered against the reigning
system. These councils, after their convention on
May 5, 1789, set about reforming the taxes and loans,
instead of creating new ones. But on this matter the
nobles and the clericals had somewhat different views
from the bourgeoisie. These were victorious through

their hostile attitude towards these councils. The general councils were formed into a constituent National Assembly, which gave France an entirely new constitution.

The power of the National Assembly was at first only a moral power. It reposed in the consciousness that by far the great majority of the nation was behind it. But that by no means sheltered it against a *coup d'etat* of a physical order. The monarchy still had at its command such power—the army, for instance—and it was quite prepared to make use of it if necessary.

But they had to bear in mind the physical strength which still lay at the disposal of Paris. It was only when Paris had been overcome that they dared to hope to dismember the National Assembly, and to bend it to its will. Hence numerous troops were marshalled together in Paris; and when it was thought that all was safe the *coup d'etat* followed, and the dismissal of the Minister, Necker, whom the National Assembly had endeavoured to force the King to accept (July 12, 1789).

Whether Paris had taken this event quite calmly or whether it had come into conflict with the troops, the fate of the Revolution would have been sealed. But Paris rose up; the King's troops failed; the proletariat and the small bourgeois masses broke into the 'Invalides,' captured some 30,000 pieces of arms, and stormed the fortress that lay before the revolutionary suburb, viz., the Bastille (July 14, 1789).

But now the King and his courtiers combined, and the peasants rose in revolt throughout the length and breadth of the land. Already before there had been instances of single peasant risings, which had been easily quelled. But now no power could withstand the storm that arose. Paris at that time saved the Revolution and made it general.

Gradually it seemed as if the storm was abating. The King and his feudal courtiers regained courage;

he began to oppose certain decisions of the National Assembly and to muster new troops. So the Parisians came to the conclusion that they could never be safe as long as the heads of the State, the King and the National Assembly, remained in Versailles. They wished to bring these under their supervision and direct influence. On October 5, 1789, large bands of people tramped to Versailles and fetched the King back to Paris. The people now hoped to have peace, and to be able to devote their energies to the building up of the constitution and to practical work, from which they expected, as a consequence of improved conditions, to derive advantage and benefit. On July 14, 1790, Louis XVI. swore fidelity to the constitution, although much against his will. He felt himself a prisoner in the Tuileries, and all the acts of his Government were repugnant to him.

Not a year had passed, since his taking of the oath to the constitution, when he secretly fled (June 21, 1791), and was misguided enough, before he had reached safety, to explain himself to the masses of the people. He left behind a document in which he declared that all his orderings and decrees since October, 1789, had been wrung from him against his will, and that he pronounced them null and void. This was a very premature move on his part; for while in flight he was recognised, taken prisoner, and brought back to Paris.

Even at that time a large section of the embittered masses demanded the dethronement of the King; but the monarchical instincts of the masses of the people were too deep-seated to make such a step successful. But it saved Louis, for at that moment it was only dethronement with which he was threatened.

He had worse fate when France, under his monarchy, became involved in war with the allied monarchies of Europe (April, 1792). This was not a war, like the preceding, for more or less land. It was a war of the feudal nobility and of European Absolutism against a people that had gained its freedom, and which was now in danger of coming under the yoke once more. It was a real civil war, with all the attendant cruelties that characterise civil wars. The country's enemy threatened the revolutionary people with total destruction, and their own King was an ally of the country's enemy.

In this situation the monarchical idea lost all its power; nevertheless the National Assembly could not yet decide to discard it. It was the Parisians who again insisted that Louis should be taken captive and a new National Assembly convened, called the Convention, which should give France a new republican constitution (August 10, 1792). In the first sitting this new Convention unanimously decided on the abolition of the monarchy (September 21, 1792). But the Parisians believed that the safety of the Republic would not be ensured so long as Louis XVI. still lived. They demanded that he should be put on trial for treason. The majority of the Convention recoiled before this measure. But the rage of the Parisians was irresistible when they heard that a secret cupboard in the Tuileries had been discovered containing a series of documents. These documents proved that the King had bought over a number of Parliamentarians, among them Mirabeau; and that a number of his guards, who had fought in the ranks of the Austrians against France, had even during that war drawn payment from him.

In spite of all, a section of the Convention endeavoured to save the King. They wanted to appeal to the people of France. Through a general election Louis's fate was to be determined.

This attempt to play off the Provinces against Paris met with most determined opposition on the part of the Parisians. Fear of them over-ruled the Convention. The appeal to the people was rejected by 423 votes against 276. Thus was Louis' fate settled, and he mounted the scaffold on January 21, 1793.

The Republican Party that pleaded most for the King at the time were the so-called Girondists, who had derived their name from the fact that the candidates who first formed the nucleus of the party had been elected in the Province of the Gironde. They were the most furious haters of Paris, whose power they wished to break. They wanted France to become a Federal State.

" Four days after the opening of the Convention, the Girondist, Lasource, amid the applause of his confederates, reiterated the words :—" And I will not have Paris led by a band of intriguers, nor let her become for France what Rome at one time was for the Roman Empire. The influence of Paris must be reduced to the 83rd part, to that share which every other province has equally." (Kumow " The Parties in the Great French Revolution," page 349).

The opposition between the Girondists and Paris assumed the wildest forms. In the revolts of May 31 to June 2, 1793, the Parisians succeeded in carrying out their demand for the expulsion and arrest of thirty-four Girondists. The answer to this was the murder of Marat by the Girondiste, Charlotte Corday, of Normandy (July 13) and soon after the attempt by the Girondists to instigate Normandy, Brittany and the South of France against the Convention—all this during the war. Whereupon the Parisians retaliated, and they carried out (on October 31) the execution of all the Girondists who could be found in Paris.

CHAPTER IV.

The First Paris Commune.

The Paris Proletariat and its Fighting Methods.

HITHERTO we have always spoken of the " Parisians." Naturally not the whole population of Paris is to be included under this head, for there were many classes in sharp contrast to one another. By the " Parisians " the great mass of the population in the capital was to be understood, viz., the small bourgeoisie and the proletariat.

Under the latter we must not think of the modern proletarian, who is the outcome of gross industry. Certainly there were some manufacturers in Paris; but the largest section of their workmen was either engaged in service of the most varied kind as labourers and porters, or it formed a body of artisans' apprentices, who hoped one day themselves to become independent artisans. Besides these, there were countless small labourers as home workers, as well as middle-men of all kinds, who lived in bitterest poverty and the most wretched insecurity.

This poverty and insecurity made the *social* position *proletarian*; whereas by their *class* position, i.e., according to the sources of their income, they were small bourgeois, whose ideal was a comfortable bourgeois existence. Nothing is more misleading than the confusion between position according to income and position according to class. This confusion was made by Lassalle, and is being made to-day by those of our Russian comrades, who believe that the poor peasant has other class interests than the rich peasant, and has the same class interest as the wage-earning proletariat of the towns. This is just as false as the conclusion of those who believe that the small capitalists have other class interests than the large capitalists, and that their opposition to the capital of finance goes together with the class opposition of the proletariat to capital. The small capitalists wish to become big capitalists, the small peasantry also wish to increase their property—this, and not a *Socialist* society is their object. The former just as much as the latter wish to increase their income at the expense of the workmen, the small peasants through low wages and long working hours, the small capitalists through high prices for food.

The poor elements in Paris, therefore, at the time of the great revolution were, according to their class position, small bourgeois, in spite of the proletarian conditions of their existence.

These conditions gave them no objects which were different from those of the better-placed small bourgeois, although they gave them means for the growing struggle which were less sympathetic to the more prosperous small bourgeois.

The starving man cannot wait. He is in despair, and, therefore, does not stop to consider his choice of means. For him little attaches to life; he has nothing to lose save his bonds, and he, therefore, risks everything during the time of an upheaval, which shall prepare for new conditions of things, and in which he hopes to gain the world.

Thus it was the proletariat, the great mass of the population of Paris, which formed the great driving power in the Revolution. Their desperate incon-siderateness made them masters of Paris, made Paris the ruler of France. and let France triumph over Europe.

Their fighting means lay in armed insurrection. Their risings were not unprepared, nor did they spring them-selves from out of the prevailing conditions. They

were much more organised   Still, they did nevertheless arise from the spontaneous pressure of the masses,
not of their leaders ; and it was only through the masses
that these risings were often irresistible in their force.
An upheaval, which has to be fomented by the leaders,
instead of these latter being forced from below, is a
sign that the necessary driving force is wanting, and
that the whole movement is doomed to failure.
During the whole time of the growth of the Revolution, it was the masses who were the driving force, the
leaders the driven.   While this lasted things moved
forward.   When the contrary happened, and the
leaders found it necessary to incite the masses to fight.
the Revolution was already in decline.

But if an upheaval can reckon on success only when
it is spontaneous, and not initiated by the leaders, this
is not to say that it has the best chance of winning
when it is not organised.   The Paris insurrections of
the Great Revolution had their foundations in the
organisation of the masses.

Even in the first signs of disturbance, in the
storming of the Bastille, there were already nuclei for
organisation.   Later they received closer and more
permanent foundation.

In the Revolution each community claimed for itself
the greater independence.   The Constitutional
Assembly by the law of December 22, 1789, established the conditions which, in consequence of the
sudden loss of power on the part of the State, had
everywhere come into being.   The communities
acquired a high level of self-administration, viz., the
control of the whole of the local police and the command of the citizen guard, as well as of the National
Guard, which was being formed in the towns.

But at the same time the bourgeoisie strove to keep
the lower classes from sharing in their measure of
power.   The National Assembly made the fine
distinction between active and passive citizens. Active

were those who paid a direct tax on at least three days' wages. They alone had the vote for the local council and for the National Assembly. From them alone the National Guard was recruited. These bodies afterwards developed into representative associations of the moneyed classes.

But in Paris the " passive " citizens organised also, as well as their friends from the ranks of the active citizens, along with the official local representative council. They armed themselves in their own way.

For the purposes of voting Paris was divided into 60 districts, which had to select the candidates. After these had been named, the districts disappeared. But they nevertheless remained, and became organised on their own initiative as permanent institutions of the municipal administration. They would not suffer repression, and at the time when before July 14 (the storming of the Bastille) all Paris was in a state of upheaval, they began to arm the people, and to act as independent authorities. After the conquest of the Bastille the districts had already become acknowledged institutions of the municipal administration In order to come to some understanding, a central bureau was opened, where special delegates could come together, and have mutual exchange of thought. In this way there arose the first attempt at a Commune—the result of a movement upwards by means of a uniting of the district organisations, which in revolutionary fashion had come about through the initiative given by the people. While the National Assembly was gradually undermining the power of the King, the districts and then the sections gradually enlarged their sphere of activity among the people. They established the connection between Paris and the provinces, and prepared the ground for the revolutionary Commune of August 10.

(Kropotkin, " The French Revolution," 1, pages 174-179. In accordance with his anarchistic standpoint, Kropotkin has given special importance to the history of the Commune in the Revolution. Apart from special works, his books afford the best study of this history. As a consequence, he treats the Parliamentary activity at the time far less satisfactorily.)

The National Assembly tried to put an end to the District Councils. Through the law of May 27, 1790, the division of the constituencies in Paris was altered. But the " passive " citizens ignored the veto. The sections were now the central point of revolutionary activity. Soon there was no communal or State question which was not taken over by these sections, and in the settling of which they were not actively concerned. The result of this was that the general assembly of these sections became a permanent institution. It was only through the permanency of their nature that intensive activity could be developed.

On August 10, 1792, the sections entirely superseded communal representation, which had already become totally effete, and they formed something new, the revolutionary Commune, to which each section sent three commissioners. Thenceforward, it was this Paris Commune which, supported by these sections, determined the course of the revolution.

The subsequent works on history have failed to give the sections their due. Their work was performed by the nameless many. The great names of the Revolution shone more in the Club of the Jacobins than in the sections. But what the Club achieved owed its success to the sections, and often it was the Club which was the part that hesitated and hung back. Only the proletariat, which had nothing to lose, was able to rush without hesitation boldly into the unknown.

THE ORIGINS OF THE REGIMENT OF TERROR.

Through the Commune the proletariat of Paris arrived at a dominating position in revolutionary France. But this position was a divided one, like the position of Paris in the country, and like that of the proletariat of that time in general society.

Small bourgeois according to their class-consciousness, they adopted the point of view of private property as against the means of production. They could not get rid of private property, they needed it in order to go on producing and live. Yet their attitude as poor wretches was one of hostility to the property of the rich, whose prosperity angered them, and whose wealth arose from their misery. It was this very recklessness towards the great feudal and capitalist property which gave them that energy in fighting the counter-revolution, and which, thanks to the pre-eminent position of Paris, made them pioneers of the Revolution, in which the great bulk of the nation took such active interest. In their powerful struggles against feudalism and the monarchy in France, and against the whole monarchical system of Europe, the revolutionary proletariat of Paris had behind it the whole strength of the nation. the most powerful nation in the world. As a result they were able to defy the men in power all the world over; indeed, the power of these men came into their hands. It was during that time that the powerful revolutionary self-consciousness of the Paris workman came into being. Through it he became the much admired type of the whole fighting international proletariat up to the days of the second Paris Commune, and even up to the closing decades of the last century

Yet this very class represented the worst consumers of Paris, for they imperatively demanded cheap foodstuffs, and never more than in the days of the great revolution, which, in the literal sense of the word, could be called a famine revolt. In consequence, the poor of Paris were drawn into increasing conflict with the peasants, the middlemen, the moneyed people, with those elements in fact which, by reason of their private property, came off best in regard to the means of production, since the abolition of private property was impossible owing to the system of retail dealing then prevalent, nor was any such abolition attempted or even proposed. When in regard to this antithesis the proletarians tried to show their power in Paris, and the power of Paris over the provinces, they were made to realise that they could not for long as a minority maintain themselves against the majority. So they went to pieces in spite of their former triumphs.

The proletarians went into the Revolution expecting to banish all misery by getting rid of the misery of feudalism, in the same way as the bourgeoisie had promised and meant. They now seized political freedom and power, and still it was only the bourgeois and the peasant who arrived at any measure of prosperity. Poverty in the large towns was not diminished; on the contrary, the real pinch of poverty first began to make itself really felt.

Starvation and a rise in prices are the outstanding features of the whole time of revolution. They are generally explained as being due to the fact that a number of bad harvests followed in succession. To me, however, it seems that the starvation during the Revolution was not due to this alone, but was a direct consequence of the Revolution itself.

Production among the peasants was at that time, to a high degree, self-sufficing. The peasant had scarcely any need of the industrial products of the town, except for articles of luxury. He produced not only his own food-stuffs, but also the raw materials for textile industry which he himself manufactured. He also constructed his own simple furniture and many of his household tools, whatever else he needed in the industrial line was furnished him by village workmen. The fact that, in spite of this, he did sell his produce in the town was due not to his own industrial needs, but to the taxes with which the State had burdened him.   He could not pay these if he did not bring to market his corn, cattle, wine, or whatever else he produced at home.

Besides all this, he had to pay his feudal lord in kind, as well as to perform a certain amount of forced labour on his lord's estate.   Of the land products, which these feudal lords thus amassed, only a small portion was used for home consumption ; the greater part they sold, in order to get money for a life of pleasure in the town.

Taxes and feudal obligations therefore provided the monies, on the one hand, which flowed into Paris and there reached circulation ; they also provided, on the other hand, the produce which was sold for bare cash to provision Paris.

The Revolution temporarily put an end to feudal obligation, as well as to taxes, as the State had no power to collect these.   The peasants were therefore no longer in such necessity to sell as they were before.   In the first place, they made use of their newly-gained freedom to eat to their fill, and to put an end to the starvation conditions, to which State and Feudalism had condemned them.   What remained over of their produce they decided to sell, only at very high prices. Nothing henceforward forced them to sell cheaply. For that reason alone a rise in prices and a contrast between Paris and the Provinces was bound to arise, and this contrast assumed an exaggerated form.   In 1793 the Convention had actually formed a revolutionary army of 10,000 men, whose duty it was to scour the villages and requisition food for Paris, in a similar way to that recently tried in Russia, and with equal failure.   This is one of the features that makes the Russian Revolution of to-day assume great resem-

blance, even in external matters, to the great bourgeois
Revolution of the 18th century.

The contrast was made even more drastic by the war,
which led to France's being " encircled," and which
hindered the lack of provision from being mitigated by
any import from without. It made the Parisians suffer
still more from hunger, and loaded the country people
with heavy war burdens, in the shape of universal
conscription.

The Parisians had the strongest motives for desiring
victory. They, as a revolutionary centre, would have
been the first to feel defeat. Moreover in Paris
national feeling was strongest developed. On the
greatness and the strength of the Empire directly
depended the greatness and strength of Paris. The men
of the " Mountain," of the extreme left of the Convention coined the phrase—"the one indivisible Republic,"
and the word " Patriot " soon had the significance of
radical revolutionary.

Utterly different was the attitude of the peasants
towards the war. Those on the frontier certainly
wanted to be rid of a foreign invasion, and they of all
others were most threatened with the return of feudal
bondage through a foreign victory. They, therefore,
felt as patriotic as the Parisians. That was especially
true of the Alsatians. It was different for those who
were far removed from the frontier, and thus were not
threatened by foreign invasion. These peasants did
not grasp the political import of the war. They only
felt the burdens of war which, according to them, were
imposed on them by the regicidal and godless Parisians.
Such provinces as La Vendée, Normandy and
Brittany, under certain circumstances, could go so far
in their opposition to Paris as to proceed to an open
revolt, whenever they could get the necessary leadership. This was provided from time to time by the
anti-revolutionary aristocrats. But the revolutionary
bourgeois also embodied in the Girondistes, once

attempted a similar revolt of the provinces against Paris, as we have already seen.

The financiers likewise came along with the peasants into conflict with the proletarians and the small bourgeois. Indeed, the opposition was even more pronounced, and had even more direct consequences. It was not an opposition between workmen and industrial capitalists, who at the time did not play a very large part. Even after the Revolution St. Simon reckoned these latter among the working classes. It was the opposition to moneyed and trade capital, to usurers, speculators, dealers and sellers. These men did not themselves cause the lack of provisions, but they exploited the calamity and increased the stress. We need not dwell on this. We ourselves have had terrible experience of this for the last five years.

During this time of misery, profiteering caused by high prices became grossly provocative. Along with this was to be classed the profiteering of the war contractors—since 1792—as well as of those who speculated in land. The National Assembly had confiscated church possessions—perhaps a third of the French landed property.

In addition to this, the aristocratic emigrants, who had fled from France in order to fight the revolution from without, were likewise deprived of their property. Their land was also confiscated. Yet all this enormous property did not remain in the possession of the State, nor was it divided among the poor peasants, but sold up. This, in the first instance, was the result of the low state of finance, which gave the final blow that caused the Revolution. But the Revolution did not raise the state of finance; on the other hand, it was depreciated, because the peasants could no longer pay their taxes. Often those who made a profit out of the selling of confiscated land-property would buy new tracts of land at a low price, solely with the intention of parcelling them up and selling them in small sections

at a high price. The financial difficulties of the State
were little helped by this means, but the speculators in
property flourished exceedingly.

In her necessity there was no other means open to
the State than the issue of revolutionary paper money.
This soon began to grow to an enormous extent.
Hence a new cause of high prices arose, as well as a
cause for extraordinary fluctuation of exchange and
prices, which state of affairs was again turned to their
own advantage by the speculators and moneylenders.

Thus there grew up from among the ruins of the old
feudal system of property a new capitalistic system,
which grew, along with the general distress, in proportion as the proletariat rose to power. This strange
situation showed clearly enough how little the mere
possession of political power is able to affect the working of economic laws, so long as the necessary social
conditions are lacking. Nevertheless the proletariat of
Paris was hungry.

They did not examine what, under the given
economical conditions, was possible and what was
inevitable. They were in power, and determined to
make the most of it, in order to arrive at that Utopian
state of equality and brotherhood and of general
prosperity, which the intellectuals among the
bourgeoisie had promised them. As they could not
alter the process of production, they tried by the help
of coercive means to change the results of this process
—means of which our own days have given us more
than enough, viz., high prices, compulsory loans, which
corresponded roughly to our war-credit and similar
measures. All of these, however, were less capable of
diminishing the distress than they are to-day, on
account of the scattered production, the lack of
statistics, and the paralysing of the central power in its
relation to the districts, which existed at that time.

As time went on, the contradiction between the
political strength of the proletariat and its economical

situation became greater. And along with this the oppression caused by the war became worse. Hence the rulers among the proletariat in their despair turned more and more to outward methods, to bloody intimidation and terrorism.

THE FAILURE OF TERRORISM.

Through the Commune the revolutionary bourgeois and proletariat of Paris ruled the whole of France. But they took care not to exercise their power directly, and to give as their watchword :—" All power to the Commune." They knew that the Empire was to be held together and ruled only by an Assembly that represented the whole Empire. They therefore avoided touching on the convention in the National Assembly. They maintained their power not *without* the Convention nor even *against* it, but *through* it.

Lenin must have formed a similar plan, otherwise it would be difficult to discover why he convoked the constitution, instead of allowing votes for it to be taken. Yet the Commune was more fortunate than he ; for it understood how to make use of this important instrument, which Lenin on the very first day unwillingly cast aside.

Certainly the " mountain " in the Convention, which went hand in hand with the Commune, was in the minority ; nevertheless, the majority was not made up of politicians of strong character and firm conviction. Many of them proved to be uncertain and hesitating. They allowed themselves to be influenced by the Paris milieu ; and where that was not strong enough to cause them to vote with the " mountain " it was sufficient to place energetic pressure on them, to make them vote as was desired.

By means of these molluscs, of this " bog," the " Mountain " was able to occupy a majority in the Convention.

Yet in the stress of time, which often demanded swift measures, the legislating activity of the Convention was not always satisfactory. And even the laws proved to be ineffectual to cope with social need and necessity. Every oppressive law, be it never so strict, puts limitations on its sphere of activity, if only for the reason that it enjoins certain rules which give the oppressed occasion and opportunity, with a little skill, to turn them to their own advantage. This policy of oppression, which is directed against phenomena that are closely bound up with existing relations and are therefore ineradicable, is obliged sooner or later to liberate itself from the shackles of laws which itself has formed, and to have recourse to lawless oppression and finally to *Dictatorship*.

This, and this alone, is the real meaning of the word Dictatorship: it is a *form of government*, not merely a *state of affairs*. It represents arbitrary force, which by its very nature can be put into practice by one person alone, or only by a very small circle of persons, knowing how to operate without any formal conditions, or willing to be led by one man alone. To ensure collaboration, every large circle requires definite rules, an administration, etc.—in other words, it is already bound by laws.

The type of dictatorship as a form of government lies in *personal* dictatorship. Class-dictatorship is pure nonsense. Class-rule without laws and regulations is unthinkable.

Since the repressive measures against profiteers, speculators and counter-revolutionaries hopelessly failed, the proletarian element had recourse to a dictatorship.

As early as March 25th, 1793, the Convention had to form a " Committee of Public Safety and General

Defence," which gradually acquired the powers of an absolute autocracy, whose members were very small in number. At first this Committee consisted of 25, which number was afterwards reduced to 9. All consultations were secret. It controlled ministers and generals, appointed and dismissed officials and officers. It dispatched commissioners with unlimited powers and could take whatever measures it regarded as necessary. These measures had to be carried out by the ministers without question. It was indeed responsible to the National Assembly, but this was a mere formality, as that body literally trembled before the Committee. Restrictions were laid on the powers of this Committee to some extent at least; for it was ordained that the Committee should be re-elected each month, and that it should have no control over the State treasury. Soon this "Committee of Public Safety" became the exclusive organ of the "Mountain." But the more the dictatorial orderings of this body increased the greater became the dictatorial power of a single personality in their midst, viz., Robespierre.

As further instruments of the dictatorship two other institutions were created: (a) a Police Committee, called the Committee of General Security, and (b) the Extraordinary Revolutionary Tribunal, which had to adjudge in all cases of counter-revolutionary activity, and of attacks on the liberty, equality and inviolability of the Fatherland.

To be suspected and denounced by a "Patriot" was sufficient for a man to be condemned to death, and indeed without any chance of appeal.

Louis Blanc, in his "History of the French Revolution," has given the following account of the organisation of the Reign of Terror.

"We find a tireless Club, that of the Jacobins, which animated Paris with its life.

"Paris, which has been divided up into groups of

c

inhabitants called ' Sections,' gives expression to the ideas and thoughts prevailing in the Club.

" The Commune, the centre of the ' Sections, formulates these ideas and thoughts into laws.

" The ' Committee of Public Safety ' infuses life into these laws in all the various departments of State activity—in the State administration, in the choice of officials, in the army, through the commissioners; in the provinces, and in every part of the Republic, through the revolutionary committees.

" The ' Committee of Public Security ' has the task of exposing all objectionable and disagreeable elements.

" The extraordinary Revolutionary Tribunal hastens to punish them.

" Such was the revolutionary machine."

(" Histoire de la Revolution Française, Bruxelles, 1856, II. p. 519.")

In the most unsparing manner this fearful apparatus was set to work.

It was hoped, by this means, to get the better of the smugglers, the extortioners, and speculators, especially if smugglers, extortioners and speculators were summarily beheaded.

But the economical situation was less calculated than ever before to encourage the belief, that in manual labour of any kind lay a gold-mine. And more than ever before each individual became a victim of the worst misery, in the larger towns at least, if he had money, and a good deal of money, at his disposal. The Regiment of Terror did not shrink from striving for gold, only it strove to get what it coveted by underhand methods. Hence a new source of self-enrichment, and corruption arose in the form of bribery.

The more dangerous it became to be caught, the more inclined were the people " wanted " to buy off and silence the exposer of their misdeeds by appropriate offers of part of their spoils. And the greater the misery, the greater was the temptation on the part of individual bodies of the revolutionary administration to make a source of profit out of shutting their eyes.

In this way, despite the furious activity of the guillotine, new property was being accumulated, and other capitalists grew up in the place of those who had been beheaded; nor did hunger and famine diminish.

These new capitalists sprang up direct from the small bourgeoisie, the proletariat, and the ranks of the revolutionaries, with whom they proved themselves to be among the most desperate and the most cunning, by no means, however, among those of strongest character. But the best elements among the revolutionaries, the disinterested, and the most self-sacrificing were, at the same time, involved in continual struggles at the frontier, as well as in civil wars. Thus the ranks of the revolutionary proletariat were depleted from two sides through the death of the best elements, and the gradual appearance of the most vicious and hardened among them in the class of adventurers. It lost on both sides its most energetic members. The remainder became more and more apathetic and discouraged. The revolution had been going on for four years; it had brought the peasants and the financiers privileges, even wealth; but for the proletariat, who had fought with most energy and self-sacrifice, and who ultimately succeeded in uniting in their hands the power of France, the revolution had nothing to offer. It did not even satisfy their hunger; on the contrary, it increased it. Even the bloody regiment of terror fared no better. What had it indeed to expect from politics? Doubt, distrust and exhaustion began to make their presence felt amongst them.

It soon came to pass that the ruling powers in the Paris Commune had vast demands to settle. We have seen already that the power of the various " sections " consisted in the fact that all citizens took permanent

active interest in their doings. Moreover, these sections were meeting uninterruptedly, and themselves
had to settle all matters connected with administration
and political action. But as time went on that
became impossible; the proletarians and the small
bourgeoisie had to be productive in their labours. How
otherwise were they to live? With occasional work,
which might at any moment be broken off, they could
not proceed very far. So long as the revolutionary
fire glowed within them, and so long as they hoped
to derive economic benefit from a revolutionary policy,
they endeavoured to make the best of their conditions.
The more they began to doubt, the more they sought
salvation in productive labour, instead of in politics.
They became more and more willing to allow one
department after another to pass into the hands of the
various sections. They allowed these sections to
appoint State-paid officials, whereby the bureaucratic
centralisation of the Empire, which was to come later,
was gradually introduced. At the same time, the
prosperous people and their followers in the sections,
to whom they made payments in some form or other,
soon outnumbered the others; for the simple reason
that they were men of leisure and could find time to
meet, whereas the proletarians and the small bourgeois, who were bound to work for a living, appeared
less and less at the meetings. Hence, there was a
danger that the former should gain the majority over
the latter.

A sign of the decline of revolutionary activity in the
sections is furnished by the decision of the Convention,
given on September 9, 1793, which limited the number of sittings to two in the week, and granted to each
member, who had to work for his living, the sum of
two francs for each sitting. But this did not check
the growing slackness in attendance.

Along with this there was also a marked change in
the relations between the masses and their leaders.

During the period when the revolution was on the increase, it was the masses who urged on the leaders, inspiring them with energy and confidence in victory. Such is the proper relation between the masses and the leaders, whenever and wherever any popular movement is to meet with success. The leaders will always display more hesitancy than the masses, whenever a revolution is in progress; because they, more than the masses, can take better account of possible eventualities, and see better than they the difficulties that are bound to arise.

But this time the leaders were in a position in which they needed renewed energy on the part of the masses if they were to maintain themselves and not be completely submerged. For the masses were becoming exhausted, and began more and more to doubt and despair. So it fell to the leaders to spur on the people, to rouse and inspire them. Such a condition of things always betokens in any popular movement that the inward strength is lacking, that it has not yet acquired that strength, or has lost it already.

In order to encourage the people, the regime in power had to give the appearance of possessing strength; it was obliged to intoxicate them and thus make them oblivious of the want of social and economic success. This effect was best obtained by inciting the lust for blood. So this was a further reason for continuing the system of Terrorism, indeed, for increasing it and making it more effective. Finally, the growing nervousness of the men in power, occasioned by the feeling they had that the ground was slipping away from under their feet, helped materially to the same result. With the desperation that followed, the bitterness increased, not only against those who were enjoying class privilege, but also against members of their own faction, who held the same general principles as they, though differing in minor details. Thus those in power felt with increasing misapprehension that every mistake and every false step would eventually lead to ruin.

It is significant of the rise of a revolution that it proceeds on its way unhindered by any piece of folly that may have been enacted. In a state of decline, on the contrary, a revolution may feel the dire effects of the slightest error.

The more precarious the position of the leaders of the Revolution became, the more bitterly did the different groups quarrel among themselves; hence the more imperative did it seem to each one of them to suppress the other, in order to save the Revolution.

Among the men of the "Mountain" there had been at the very outset marked differences between the "believers" (if not actually practising "church-believers") and atheists; between the Philistine Puritans and the cynical epicureans, between the inconsiderate and the considerate. But this did not prevent their harmoniously working together. When these different groups began to attack one another, with such rage as to employ the "Regiment of Terror" as a means of suppression one against the other, that was already a sign of the decline of the Revolution. The fate of the Revolution was already sealed when Robespierre's faction dragged before the revolutionary tribunals the Hebertistes, as being "Ultra-revolutionary" and the Dantonists for being "corrupt" and "too moderate," and succeeded in making them share the same fate on the guillotine (March, 1794) which they had prepared for the Girondists some months before.

These terrorist measures were already a sign of the downfall of the Revolution; they further aided it by causing the masses in the Paris Commune to split, thus turning the disciples of the guillotined into enemies of the revolutionary government. At the same time, and as a result of the growing apathy of the masses, the government was obliged to withdraw the various functions, hitherto assumed by the sections, from those bodies, and to transfer them to the State officials.

The police, and in particular the political police, fell into the hands of the two central bodies, who really had the State power in their own hands, and they were the Committee of Public Safety and the Committee of Security of the Convention. The police became an all-powerful instrument of an almighty government, and at the same time it changed from being one of the institutions of the various sections, which functioned in full publicity, into one wholly secret in character. The secret police thus became an invisible power, which was supreme over everything else in the State.

But all the efforts of the leaders to save themselves by terrorist means were frustrated. The ground on which they stood began to shrink from under their feet. They could only, as a last resort, increase the system of terrorism and the police power. But the sole result was that, as they all felt their position to be more and more threatened, they banded themselves together in a desperate attempt to withstand opposition; since in the decisive moments these rulers had nobody to support them.

Kropotkin, an enthusiastic admirer of the Paris Commune in the Revolution, and therefore one who would be anything but an opponent of that institution, has well described the fatal path that terrorism was bound to take. In the 67th chapter of his book on the French Revolution, entitled "Terrorism," he makes the following remarks: "The darkest feature (apart from the war without) was the attitude of the provinces, especially in the South. The wholesale massacres, practised without any distinction, against the counter-revolutionary leaders, as well as against those whom they led and organised by the local Jacobins and delegates of the Convention, had engendered such profound hatred that it now became a question of war to the knife. And the position became increasingly difficult, since nobody, whether in the locality or in Paris, could proffer any more salutary advice than a resort to the extremest means of revenge."

He quotes incidents in proof of his statement, and then shows how Robespierre felt himself compelled to push terrorism to the extreme. Louis Blanc believes that Robespierre himself wished to detach himself from the system of terrorism, the pernicious results of which he foresaw and keenly felt. But he could find no other way of getting the better of the men within his own ranks, who were sworn to terrorism, than by fighting them by terrorist means in their most aggravated forms. Louis Blanc says: "Robespierre wanted to make those men tremble who themselves had made the whole world tremble before them. He conceived the bold plan of felling them with their own battleaxes, and of crushing terrorism by means of terrorism itself." (History of the French Revolution, II., page 748).

It is a disputable point, whether such were Robespierre's motives or not. Certain it is, however, that he himself forced through the decree of the 22 Prairial (June 10th, 1794), which removed altogether the last vestiges of legal security accorded to political suspects. In the Revolutional Tribunal the defenders of such suspects were removed, and the legal procedure was carried out according to the dictates of "sane human reason" alone. The verdict depended on the "judge's conscience" and on his "mediatory powers," whatever they might be.

As early as February 24th, 1794, Robespierre had declared: "They are trying to govern the revolution by means of chop-logic. Trials of conspiracy against the Republic are conducted as if they were trials between private persons. Tyranny kills and liberty pleads in its defence. And the penal code, which the conspirators themselves have drawn up, is the very system according to which they themselves are condemned."

The only punishment that was to be recognised was the death penalty. It was to be meted out even to those '' who had disseminated false news, with intent to cause dissension or confusion among the people, who aimed at undermining the moral status or attempted to poison the public conscience." By such measures every government can instantly silence opposition. Kropotkin, referring to this, says: '' To promulgate this decree meant nothing less than declaring the bankruptcy of the revolutionary government. Thus the effect of this decree of the 22 Prairial was to bring the counter-revolution to full maturity within the space of six weeks."

Instantly, on the strength of this decree, some 54 people were executed. '' Thus the new decree, everywhere known as Robespierre's decree, began immediately to take effect. It caused the Regiment of Terror to become at once the object of intense hatred."

Immediately there were wholesale trials of 150 suspects, who were summarily executed in three batches.

'' It is unnecessary to dilate any longer on these executions. It is sufficient to say that from April 17th, 1793, the day of the establishment of the revolutionary tribunals, up to the 22 Prairial of the year 4 (June 10, 1794), that is to say during the course of fourteen months, the Tribunal in Paris has already issued orders for the execution of 2,607 persons. But since the promulgation of the new decree the same tribunal, in the course of only 46 days, from the 22 Prairial to the 9th Thermidor (July 27th, 1794), condemned to death 1,351 persons. The people of Paris began to shudder with horror at the sight of all these executioners' carts, in which the condemned were conveyed to the guillotine, and which the five

executioners with difficulty succeeded in emptying
day by day.   Soon there was difficulty in finding
cemeteries enough to bury the dead; for on every
occasion, when a new cemetery was opened in the
working-class quarters of the city, lively protests were
made."

The sympathies of the working-class population of
Paris now turned towards the victims; the more so,
because the rich had fled, or were in hiding some-
where in France, thus leaving the poor to the mercy
of the guillotine.   As a matter of fact, among 2,750 of
the guillotined, whose status Louis Blanc was able to
verify, only 650 belonged to the wealthier classes.   It
was even whispered that on the "Committee of
Safety" was sitting a Royalist, an agent of Batz, who
instigated the executions, in order to make the Republic
hated.   Certain it is that every fresh wholesale
massacre of this kind hastened the downfall of the
Jacobin regiment.

The whole world felt itself threatened by Robespierre
and his followers.   The whole world accordingly united
together against them, "Extreme Radicals,"
"Moderates," Girondistes and Montagnards (known
as the "Mountain"), terrorists and humanists,
proletarians and bourgeois.

Robespierre's power came to an end at the first
attempt made by those whom he threatened to show
their teeth.   His appeal to the populace on the
9th Thermidor met with indifferent reception.   He
succumbed.   At the same time the Commune of Paris
lost the last apparent claim to power that it had
exercised so long.   The revolution thereupon reverted
to the basis favoured by the economic conditions then
prevailing, namely, to the supremacy of the bourgeoisie.

CHAPTER V.

The downfall of Robespierre signified the worst possible collapse. It was a moral collapse brought about by the fact that the proletarians and the small bourgeois of Paris forsook the party that represented them and refused any longer to fight for them. Indeed, they breathed freely as if they had been relieved of some heavy burden, when finally an end was put to the fearful massacres.

But this deplorable end was soon forgotten. What remained deeply rooted in the memories of the revolutionary proletarians and small bourgeois—not only in Paris—was the remembrance of the great and splendid time, when they, through their insurrections, dominated the Convention, and through the Convention, France itself, the mightiest State of that period, which was in a position to defy the whole of Europe, and even subjugate it, temporarily at least.

The more wretched the times for the proletariat, the small bourgeoisie, and the revolutionaries generally under the sabre-government of Napoleon, especially after his overthrow under the regiment of the "Junkers" and the financial magnates, the more did the revolutionaries cherish those great traditions.

There are very few men who study history for any scientific purpose and in a scientific spirit, that is to say, with the intention of trying to discover the causal nexus in the development of humanity, in order to bring it into line irrefutably with the whole body of recognised interconnections in this development; or in other words, in order to make their conceptions of the world and things more profound, and to arrive at clearer knowledge and stronger foundations.

The starting point of every science has always some very practical aim, and is not the result of an impulse towards philosophical knowledge. Proof of this is to be found in so abstract a science as geometry through its very name alone, which implies nothing other than the art of measuring the earth.

In like manner the starting point of history was a purely practical one. namely, the laudation of one's forefathers, in order to stimulate the rising generation to emulate them. Since it was not primarily a question of knowledge, but rather of political and ethical consequences, it was not regarded as necessary to stick absolutely to the truth. Exaggeration was readily indulged in, so that the effect might be enhanced; nor did they shrink from deliberate invention. Historical falsification is as old as the writing of history itself.

As is generally known, this method of writing and explaining history has continued up to the present day. It is regarded as being the manifestation of great patriotic feeling—much more than any praiseworthy accomplishment.

The writing of history has a further practical object. It was a means of establishing the claims of separate states, or of separate localities, clans or families, within a State, through the customs, agreements or treaties of bygone days. This brand of historical exposition gave the falsifier rich material. Thus a great part of the wealth and power of the Catholic Church, as well as of the Pope and individual bishops, orders and monasteries, was established on falsified documents.

The fabrication of false documents has gone out of fashion, since reading and writing have ceased to be confined to a few chosen circles. That, however, " Historical Science " always understands very well how to produce, at pleasure, established proofs in support of every historical claim to any legal right, has been abundantly shown to us by the skill with which every belligerent land in the last few years has produced " scientific " proofs of its historical rights, corresponding to its appetites and desires.

Nevertheless the most important advantage to be derived from history lies neither in the inspiration and enthusiasm to be derived from contemplating the exploits and brave deeds of one's forefathers, nor in the establishing of claims to certain rights; but rather in the increasing of the power that belongs to him who wishes to derive benefit from experiences made in the past.

This increase of power may take a double form. On the one hand the individual can augment his intellectual power, by *learning* something from history. That is to say, that he examines the successes and failures of his predecessors, and attempts to discover what he himself might have done, or left undone, in given circumstances. Especially in military matters the knowledge derived from history has had enormous practical results. There has hardly ever been an army leader who has not wandered through the history of war, and learnt from his predecessors.

More difficult is the knowledge of political matters to be derived from a study of history. Far greater masses come under consideration in the question of politics than in the case of war, especially in the wars of earlier times And these masses are not will-less instruments in the hand of an all-powerful leader, but very individual and to be tackled with difficulty. And finally, the relations with which a politician has to deal are much more varied and changeable than in the case of military matters. Even in military matters, which embrace relations of simpler order, more easy to survey than politics, it would be fatal if learning from history should lead to an unintelligent imitation of the past, rather than to a purposeful application of the general rules and principles, derived from the study of history, to the particular case. In politics the differences in the social conditions and situations of the individual countries and times are much greater, and therefore much less easy to recognise. Hence an imitation, according to pattern, of the events of the past, applied directly to situations which merely bear superficial resemblance to events of the past, can often do more harm than good and cloud the vision, rather than brightening it, in its quest for the knowledge of the true state of affairs and of the particular needs of the moment.

What happens, then, in politics is that men have little understood how really to learn. But most politicians, even when they do busy themselves with historical knowledge, are far less concerned about "learning" than about something quite different. And so we come to the consideration of the second means of increasing one's power and strength by a study of history.

Every one of the present-day classes and parties finds its analogy in the past; for in bygone days, as in our own, there were struggles between exploiters and the exploited, between those with possessions and those without, between aristocrats and democrats, between monarch and republicans. These classes and parties of the past were certainly governed by conditions very different from those prevailing at the present day; they often signified something quite different from the corresponding phenomena of a later period. But in politics the events of to-day are measured and compared with similar events of the past, with their successes and failures. For the sake of propaganda in a particular direction, it always added to one's power if one could refer to some event in the past, which had met with success. And it was no less addition to the strength of one's propaganda, if one could show the other side, and point out where a contrary action has led to the shipwreck of one's predecessor.

This occasioned a very keen interest in the study of history, but by no means a real interest in historical truth. Here also we find instances of the falsification of history. The writers of each party naturally seek to put their protagonists in a bright light, and their opponents in as dark a light as possible. Amid the practical needs which give rise to the falsification of history, those only are free from tendency to falsification who are animated by a desire really to learn. This desire leads to the attempt at discovering the failures, as well as the successes, of one's predecessors, and subjecting them and their actions to rigorous criticism. At this point we find the transition to the purely scientific impulse towards exact truth, towards the examination of history out of the pure desire to satisfy the demands of causality.

All other practical needs that lead to the writing of history develop the tendency to degrade the scientific, until it merely becomes a fabrication of legends. Fortunately, nowadays, the critic of the other side can always expose such trickery. This sort of business can no longer proceed in such a simple way as at the time when the gospels were collated. except under the regime of a state of siege, or under the censor. But even at the highest grade of popular education and unrestricted liberty of the Press, there is no lack of one-sided expositions of history.

Naturally it must not be supposed that there is always a conscious attempt to lead the reader astray. In most cases it is the historical writer who is led astray through his own party fanaticism and party narrowness, which generally prevent him from seeing things as they really are.

This is all the more possible, since the sources which we draw upon to supply historical information are often themselves the result of party struggle, and since social relations are always so extraordinarily complex that the most detached enquirer often experiences difficulty

in finding his way about, and must often ask himself
the question, "What is truth?"

Lissagaray rightly says, in the preface to his
" History of the Commune ": " The man who gives
the people false stories of the revolution and deceives
them, whether intentionally or not, by 'historical
fantasies,' lays himself open to punishment, as much
as a geographer who should sketch false charts for
seafarers."

And yet I know comrades in my party, thoroughly
honest and honourable comrades, who regard it as a
sacred duty towards the revolution to mislead the
people, by giving them false "historical fantasies"
about Bolshevism.

On the other hand, how difficult it is even for the
most conscientious historian, while the storm is at its
height, to indicate on a map all the dangerous rocks
which have been passed on the voyage! Revolutions,
which let loose men's passions, and in which men
fight for life or death, naturally suffer more than all
other historical events from party exposition and ideas.
And so true is this, that in the great French Revolution it was the Paris Commune, with its reign of
terror, representing the most powerful driving-force
and the most passionate manifestation of that Revolution, which was most violently combated.   It was
to this institution that the counter-revolutionaries
pointed whenever they wanted to characterise and
denounce the Revolution.   But to defend it was regarded by the revolutionaries as a duty.   They were
not content with regarding the regiment of terror as
a particular form assumed by the revolution at that
time, a form which belonged to the past, not to be
revived in the future.   They were not content with
explaining the special conditions that were responsible for the formation of that regiment.   On the contrary, they felt themselves constrained to glorify
instead of condemning that institution, regarding the

" Terror " as a horrible but necessary means for the liberation of the enslaved classes.

Even Marx himself in 1848 still reckoned on the victorious power of revolutionary Terrorism, in spite of the fact that he had at that time already criticised the traditions of 1793.

In the *Neue Rheinische Zeitung* he repeatedly spoke in favour of terrorism. In one number (January 13th, 1849) he wrote as follows concerning the rising of the Hungarians, whose revolutionary importance he over-estimated:

" For the first time in the revolutionary movement of 1848, for the first time since 1793, a nation surrounded by counter-revolutionary powers, has dared to oppose revolutionary passion to cowardly anti-revolutionary rage, and to meet white terror with red terror. For the first time for many years we find a truly revolutionary character, a man who dares to take up the gauntlet in the shape of a desperate struggle in the name of his own people, and who for that nation is Danton and Carnot in one. That man is Ludwig Kossuth."

Before that, in a number of the same journal, November 7th, 1848, Marx wrote in connection with the affair in Vienna:

" In Paris the destructive counter-stroke of the June Revolution will be overcome. With the victory of the ' Red Republic ' in Paris, the armies from the interior will spread up to and beyond the frontiers, and the actual power of the contesting parties will become evident. Then we shall think of June and of October (the overthrow of Vienna by Windischgratz), and we too shall shout: ' Vae victis.'* The futile massacres since the days of June and October, the exhaustive sacrifices since February and March, the cannibalism of the counter-revolution, will convince the people that there exists only one means of shortening, simplifying

* In the original edition this was printed in large thick letters.

and centralising the death agony of the old order of society and the bloody birth-throes of the new—only one means, and that is *Revolutionary Terrorism*."

This was not put to a practical test. But we find among the revolutionaries themselves a growing contradiction within. If a study of the past drives them to uphold terrorism, their attitude is in contradiction to their growing humanitarian instinct, arising, as we shall see later, from present-day conditions, and to their repugnance to commit acts of human torture, and even to take human life. And this humanitarianism in practice carries more weight than the obsolete terrorist creed of the history books.

Concerning the revolutionaries of July, 1830, Börne wrote in the sixth of his Paris letters: " Quickly they conquered, still quicker have they forgiven. How gentle has been the retaliation of the people who have suffered so much injury; how soon they have forgotten all! Only in open fight on the battlefield have they ever wounded the opponent. Defenceless prisoners were never murdered, fugitives never chased, those in hiding never searched for, the suspects never molested. Such is the behaviour of a people!"

In February, 1848, the Paris revolutionaries behaved as magnanimously as they had done in 1830. Even in the terrible June battle of the same year, the fighting workers exhibited the most noble heroism, and the toughest powers of endurance, but no signs of thirst for blood. This was left for their victors to develop in the most shocking manner. Not only the soldiers, whose rage was fired by invented accounts of atrocities committed by the insurgents; even the intellectuals took part in this campaign of revenge. Doctors refused to bind the wounds of wounded revolutionaries.

Marx said in this connection, in his famous article on the June battle in the *Neue Rheinische Zeitung* :

'' Science no longer exists for the plebeian, who was guilty of shameless and nameless crimes when fighting for his existence in the trenches, instead of for Louis Philippe or Marrast.''

It was indignation over such barbarities that urged Marx to write the above-cited confessions to terrorism.

The extreme bitterness, engendered by the June battle of 1848, had further consequences among the workers of Paris, when they in 1871 overcame the political power in the Second Commune.   Not a few of them had themselves taken part in the struggle of June, 1848.   It might have been expected that the days of vengeance would now come, the day of terror, prophesied by Marx.

But he himself declares in his work on the Commune ('' The Civil War in France,'' 1871):

'' From March 18th until the entry of the Versailles troops into Paris, the proletarian revolution remained innocent of all acts of violence, in which revolutionaries and especially counter-revolutionaries of the 'higher classes' are wont to revel.''   (Third edition, page 38.)

Here we find a definite repudiation of terrorism, which is regarded as a feature of the revolution of the '' higher classes,'' as compared with the proletarian revolution.

Not long ago my attitude towards Bolshevism was described as infidelity towards Marx, whose revolutionary fire would certainly have led him to Bolshevism.   As proof of this, one of Marx's declarations on the terrorism of 1848 was quoted.

We now see that the infidelity towards Marx, of which I was guilty, had been accomplished by himself as early as 1871.   Between his first and second declaration, two decades of the most strenuous and profound mental activity had intervened, the result of which was '' Capital.''

Whoever takes refuge in Marx on the question of terrorism has no right to adhere to his views of 1848

and ignore those of 1871.   Like Marx, Engels also
showed little enthusiasm in 1870 for terrorism.   On
September 4th, 1870, he wrote to Marx:

" We understand by the ' reign of terror ' the reign of
those who breathe and inspire frightfulness; on the
contrary, it is the reign of people who themselves are
frightened.   *La terreur*—this embodies for the most
part futile atrocities committed by people who themselves have fear, and have need of reassurance.   I am
convinced that the blame for the reign of terror of 1793
is almost entirely to be laid at the doors of the over-
anxious small bourgeois, who masqueraded as patriots,
and of the mob, who made of terrorism a regular business."   Correspondence between Marx and Engels,
IV., 379, 380.)

Marx was perfectly right when he, with obvious satisfaction, pointed out that the Second Paris Commune
remained free from all acts of violence, which were so
strong a feature of the First.   What did happen of a
violent nature during the time of its existence in Paris
was not to be laid to its account.   Even so, it must not
be supposed that the idea of terrorism played no part at
all in the Second Commune, or that it was repudiated
by all the members of that institution.   That was by no
means the case.

Let us now discuss this more closely, and at the same
time draw a parallel between the Paris Commune of
1871 and the Soviet Republic.   For this latter often
points to the Commune of 1871 as its prototype, and
as embodying its justification.   And Freiderich Engels,
in his preface to the third edition of Marx's " Civil
War in France," has declared that the Paris Commune represented the dictatorship of the proletariat.
Therefore it will repay us to examine this dictatorship
more closely and see what it looked like.

CHAPTER VI.

THE SECOND PARIS COMMUNE.

THE ORIGIN OF THE COMMUNE.

The Soviet Republic of 1917, like the Paris Commune of 1871, was the result of war and military defeat, and had to be borne by the revolutionary proletariat. Apart from that, a comparison with these two is at an end. The Bolsheviks succeeded in gaining political power because they, of all the political parties of Russia, were the one party which most energetically demanded peace, a peace at any price, even a separate peace. They did not worry about the general situation that might thereby arise, or whether the victory and the world supremacy of the German military monarchy might thereby be assisted or not. For a considerable time the Bolsheviks constituted themselves hirelings of the German militarists as much as the Indian or the Irish rebels and the Italian anarchists. Quite different was the attitude of French radicalism in the war of 1870, after the downfall of Napoleon and the proclamation of the Republic, and after the Germans began to make their claims of annexation of Alsace-Lorraine. In this struggle of the Third Republic against the united monarchs of Germany it seemed that the situation of 1793, with its struggle of the First Republic against the allied monarchies of Europe, would again come to life. The traditions of that earlier time again came into force, and again the proletariat of Paris formed the most warlike elements, which pursued the war in the most energetic and determined manner, for the salvation of the one and indivisible Republic.

Meanwhile the peasants of 1870 were no longer the same as those of 1793. Those of 1870 hated Paris and her supremacy. Nevertheless, they were convinced of the necessity of repelling the common enemy, since the victory of the latter would bring them again feudal exploitation, and would threaten to take from them the ecclesiastical and other property that they had acquired for themselves. The peasants of 1870, on the other hand, had nothing of a similar kind to fear from the victory of the Prussians. For them the ecclesiastical question was paramount, so that the loss of Alsace-Lorraine seemed to be the lesser evil, compared with the devastation and burden of war. Apart from the people of Alsace-Lorraine, who in desperation fought to the last moment against separation, the thought of peace gained rapid ground among the peasants and the people of the provinces as war continued. This clamour for peace arose in opposition to the radical and war-like elements of Paris, which represented the war-cry of the reactionaries and the monarchists. As in 1917 in Russia, the peace party of 1871, the party which was wearied of war, gained the upper-hand over those who wanted to continue the war. But the peace ideas in 1871 did not assist the most radical of the radicals, but on the other hand, the most reactionary among the reactionaries.

On February 8, 1871, a National Assembly was elected to conclude peace. It numbered only two hundred Republicans, and on the other hand over four hundred monarchists. "Almost the whole province demanded peace at any price. Paris, on the other hand, cried for war to the knife. She elected only those men who were pledged to the continuation of war, and who opposed a peace purchased at the price of yielding up territory." (M. Louis Debreuilh, "*La Commune*," Paris.)

On February 12th the National Assembly met in Bordeaux, and on March 1st it voted for the Peace Treaty by 516 against 117. Nearly the half of these 117 votes represented the delegates from Paris. The National Assembly was elected only with a view to the conclusion of peace. Only in consideration of this had the electors given their votes. The great majority of reactionaries in that Assembly was attributable not to the dislike of the Republic, but to the insuperable demand for peace. After this event the mandate of the National Assembly came to an end. In its place a new one had to be elected, which should decide on all matters in connection with the constitution. These votes might have turned out other than did those in the Assembly at Bordeaux, for the Republic met with less opposition than did the continuation of the war. As a matter of fact, however, the elections which took place throughout France on April 30th, 1871, gave a great Republican majority. But just because the ' junkers ' of that Party feared the National Assembly, they clung all the more tenaciously to their mandates. They formed themselves into a Constitutional Assembly, and without any doubt would have reinstated the monarchy, if they had not been split into two halves, the one half among them consisting of the legitimate supporters of the dynasty, which up to 1830, in France, had been regarded as the legitimate dynasty; and the other half being the Orleanists, the opposers of the dynasty, who, as a result of the Revolution of 1830, were placed in the position of the hereditary rulers. This split saved the Republic, yet it did not prevent Paris from being the object of the combined hatred of both factions. The French Republic had no other strong support outside Paris, but the strength of this support had proved itself on numberless occasions since 1789. There was no possibility of restoring the monarchy so long as Paris was not overcome. Provincials fought with more and more fury against Paris, against the immoral, godless, war-like Republican Paris, quite apart from its Socialism. From the very beginning of its sittings, the National Assembly gave loudest expression to its horror. Heroic Paris, which had sustained a fearful siege of over five months in the service of land defence, was now the object of the most scandalous vituperation on the part of its sublime patricians. To humiliate Paris, to deny it all self-government, to rob it of its position as the capital, and finally to disarm it in order with greater security to carry out a monarchic *coup d'état*—this was the chief concern of the National Assembly and of Thiers, its chosen Chief of Executive.

We see how utterly different this was from the *coup d'état* of the Bolsheviks, who derived their power from the desire for peace, who had the support of the peasants behind them, and who found no monarchist opposition to them in the National Assembly, but only the opposition of social revolutionaries and Mensheviks. The immediate causes of the Bolshevik Revolution and of the Second Paris Commune were as different as the results of these two movements. The Bolsheviks acquired power through a well-prepared *coup d'état*, which in one stroke yielded to them the entire State machinery, which they immediately proceeded to exploit in the most energetic and reckless manner possible, with a view to depriving their opponents of all political and economic power—of all their opponents, including the proletariat. On the other hand, at the time of the suspension of the Commune, nobody was more surprised than the revolutionaries themselves, and to a very large number of them this conflict was anything but desirable. Certainly, as the result of revolutionary tradition, the tactics of the armed insurrection, which received due preparation, were strongly supported by the Parisians. The Blanquistes were their chief representatives among the Socialists. At different times during the siege they and other elements of a Jacobin character tried to promote riots; but they could not find sufficient support, so that these attempts invariably came to nothing. As a consequence of the impression made by the capitulation of Metz on October 31st they rose and demanded the election of a Paris Representative Council, namely, the Commune, on socialist but not on patriotic grounds, in order to carry on the war more energetically than the First Paris Commune had done from 1792 to 1794. That part of the National Guard faithful to the Government succeeded in quelling this revolt without shedding blood, since the Government troops found so little opposition to overcome. In order to strengthen their position, the Government had a General Election of the people in Paris on November 3rd. As the result, there were 558,000 votes for the Government, and not quite 63,000 against. The " men of action at any price " fared no better on January 22nd. Although they opposed at the time the highly popular and patriotic voting for the continuation of the war, the Government had announced that capitulation was inevitable; and, as a result, there was an outburst of fury among the revolutionaries, which had bloodier results than the revolt of October 31st, but which, likewise, was soon crushed without difficulty.

These failures had wearied, deceived and weakened these men of action. They were not yet prepared on March 18th to call for a new revolt. On the other hand, the men of the Socialist International were, from the outset, opposed to any attempt at revolt. Immediately after the downfall of Napoleon, during the September revolution, Karl Marx wrote to Engels (September 6, 1870):—

" I had just sat down to write to you when Seraillier came in, and informed me that he would leave London for Paris on the morrow, where in any case he will stay only a day or two. His object is to arrange affairs there with the International Federal Council of Paris. This is all the more necessary, since at the present moment the whole

' French Section,' is streaming into Paris, in order
to perpetrate some folly in the name of the International. They want to overthrow the provisional
Government, to establish the Commune of Paris,
and to appoint Pyat as French Ambassador to
London, etc. I received to-day a proclamation of
the Federal Council of Paris to the German people,
which I will send you to-morrow. It contains an
urgent request to the General Council to issue a new
and special manifesto to the Germans. I had
already intended to make the same proposal this
evening. Be so kind as to send me, as soon as
possible, in English, military information about
Alsace Lorraine, which will be useful for this manifesto. I have already answered in detail the
Federal Council in Paris, and at the same time have
undertaken the disagreeable business of opening
their eyes to the real state of affairs."—(Correspondence between Engels and Marx, I. IV., p. 330.)

I have been reproved for being merely a " degene-
rate Epigone " of Marx. It is certain that Marx's
revolutionary nature and his volcanic temperament
at the time would have driven him straight into the
camp of the Bolsheviks. We see from his letter how
his volcanic temperament, at the time of the Revolution, made him regard it as his first duty to undertake
the disagreeable duty of opening the eyes of his comrades as to the actual state of affairs; and that this
same temperament, in spite of all its volcanic
character, was capable, under circumstances, of carrying out a revolutionary action, even though it was a
stupid action. Engels replied to Marx on September
7th as follows :

" Dupont has just gone. He was here this evening
and is furious over the wonderful Paris proclamation! The fact that Seraillier is going to Paris, and
that he has already spoken to you, has pacified him.
His views of the whole affair are perfectly clear and

right, namely, to turn to account the freedom which the Republic has granted for the organisation of the party in France; to take action when opportunity shall present itself after the organisation has been formed; and to restrain the International in France until peace has been made."

To this Marx replied on September 10:

"Tell Dupont that I am in entire agreement with his views."

In other words, it was *organisation*, and not *action*, which appeared the more important to his volcanic temperament. In the very fact of maintaining reserve the International in France was pursuing nothing less than a plan for precipitate action.

Let us give an example. On February 22nd, at the sitting of the Paris Federal Council of the International, a member proposed that a peaceful demonstration on February 24th should be made, on the anniversary of the Revolution of 1848. Even this peaceful demonstration appeared to the majority of the Federal Council, in view of the tense situation, highly inopportune. Frankell, in particular, opposed this suggestion. He demanded that they should devote all their strength for the moment to the organisation of the proletariat, to the study of the most important economic problems, and above all, to the payment of the wages that had become overdue during the siege, and also to the question of unemployment.

The representatives of the International in the National Assembly, Malon and Tolain, were to give expression to the will of the people. As the result of Frankell's proposal, the Federal Council decided not to arrange a demonstration, but to leave it to each individual member to decide whether he should take part in such demonstration or not. This shows no very strong leanings towards insurrection. Indeed this insurrection was engineered, not by the revolutionaries but by their opponents. As a result of the exigencies of the war, the proletariat of Paris was being formed into the National Guard, and had become armed. This state of affairs appeared to those elements that had formed round Thiers—junkers, financiers, the heads of bureaucracy and of the army —as a very grave danger. After the signature of peace, it seemed to them that nothing was so imperative as the disarmament of the proletarian section of the Paris National Guard. This was begun by their being deprived of cannon. The German rulers had caused the Paris National Guard to come into possession of these cannon; since they, the Germans, hoped that this National Guard " would be the spark to set fire to the powder magazine," as Bourgin has rightly said. (Georges Bourgin's " Histoire de la Commune," Paris, 1917, page 43.)

The thorough exploitation of victory is of the very essence of military action and science. It is part of a general's duty not only to conquer, but also to bring about the complete demobilisation and breaking up of the conquered enemy. Of a different order, however, are the aims of a statesman. He must look beyond the victory, in order to discover what conditions are possible for future relations with the momentary enemy. These two conceptions are found in opposition to one another in every crusade. The results are fatal when the military idea gains influence on politics, outside the actual prosecution of war. In the year 1866 Bismarck had already mastered and acquired the military way of thinking, if, however, with great difficulty. Yet it was the very successes of 1866 that had given the Prussian General Staff such enormous prestige, which, through the victory of 1870, increased still more. Bismarck could not oppose the Prussian General Staff. He had to yield to the military way of thinking, and as a result his own political understanding was disturbed and blinded. Hence the demand for the annexation of Alsace-Lorraine, which lengthened the war by months, which drove France into the arms of Russia, and prepared the present disruption of Germany. Nevertheless, Alsace-Lorraine was still economically and strategically a very tangible gain for the moment. But they were not content with that, but in addition tried to bring about the humiliation of Paris, that centre which the Germans so hated, because of its opposition to their armies; and they compelled France on February 26th to grant that German troops from March 1st should invade Paris and take possession of the Champs Elysées. When on February 27th this information became known to the Parisians, there arose a general cry of indignation and a call to arms, in order to throw back the common enemy by means of force. Nearly all the battalions of the National Guard declared themselves ready to follow. It was only the Internationalists who kept quiet. However disastrous for them at the moment an insurrection against an internal enemy appeared to be, no less disastrous was a rising against the enemy from without. They implored the Central Committee of the National Guard to abstain from every attempt at armed resistance, which they said would only lead to a repetition of the slaughter of the June before, and to the drowning of the Republic in the blood of the Paris workmen. They proposed that the National Guard, instead of offering armed resistance, should surround the Germans with a cordon, which would cut them off completely from the Paris population, and keep them in isolation.

The Central Committee allowed itself to be persuaded at the last moment, and so we have the International to thank that the vain arrogance of the German conquerors did not provoke the most fearful street fighting in the world's history. It was not the German but the French soldiery, which a few weeks later let loose the bloody slaughter among the Parisian proletariat.

According to the capitulation of Paris on January 28th, all war material of the troops in the town had been made over to the victor, excepting the arms of the National Guard; not only their weapons, but also their cannons, which were provided, not by the State but by the city of Paris. When, therefore, the Germans entered Paris, the Government took no steps whatever to remove to safety those cannons which, by contract, the victors had left in their care. The Government probably wished that the enemy had taken them, and thus weakened the strength of the enemy within. But the National Guard were well prepared, and brought these cannons, four hundred in number, in good time to those parts of the town to which the Germans had no access. To get back these cannons into their possession was the great anxiety of the Government after the conclusion of peace. In this way they hoped to disarm the proletarian section of the Paris National Guard. The National Guard had threatened to decapitate and decapitalise (décapiter et décapitaliser) Paris. With this end in view, they decided not to sit in Paris. With great difficulty Thiers persuaded them to make the seat of their Conference in Versailles, in the neighbourhood of Paris, instead of in Bordeaux, as had been the case up till then. On March 20th they proposed to meet there. Beforehand they had to be reassured that they had nothing to fear from Paris. Therefore it was decided to confiscate these cannon on March 18th. Thiers thought it the wisest course to steal these cannon secretly, instead of openly by force. At three o'clock in the morning, while all Paris was asleep, several regiments took possession of Montmartre, where the cannon were standing unguarded, and endeavoured to remove them. But, strangely enough, they had forgotten to bring with them the necessary horses. These therefore had first of all to be fetched; in the meantime the Parisians " smelt a rat " and, quickly gathering together, formed a continually increasing group, which finally compelled the soldiers to leave the cannon alone. They were successful. The soldiers who had lived among the Paris populace, who had fought with it against the common enemy, and had joined with it in despising the incapable generals, now fraternised with the people and the National Guard. General Lecomte, who ordered the troops to fire on unarmed crowds, merely succeeded in causing his own soldiers to turn against him, and arrest and shoot him. This shooting affray belongs to those terrorist atrocities, which one is inclined to lay to the blame of the Commune. This is also true of the shooting of General Thomas, who was seized on the morning of March 18th in civilian dress, as he was taking notes among the crowd. He was executed for being a spy. Already on the 28th of February a police agent, who was caught in the act of espionage, was thrown into the Seine and cruelly drowned.

Those people who attribute these deeds to the Commune forget that, at the time when such things happened, the Commune was not yet in existence. On the other hand, one should not lay the blame to the civil population of Paris. Each one of these executions was carried out by the soldiers, and not by the civilians. They were the outcome of the ideas, not of the proletariat but of the militarists who do not attach much importance to human life. And those friends of humanity, who wax indignant over the soldiers because they shot their bloodthirsty generals, would not have a word to say if those same soldiers had shot down women and children. "Instead of his shooting women and children, his own people shot him." (Lecomte). "Deep-rooted habits, which soldiers acquire as the result of training given them by the enemies of the working classes, do not suddenly lose their power at the moment when these same soldiers go over to the working people, and join them."—Marx, "Civil War in France," p. 38.)

Whatever action the National Guard took in these events was undertaken only with a view to prevent further bloodshed.   They succeeded, in fact, sometimes at the risk of their own lives, in rescuing from the indignant soldiers the officers they had arrested, so that only those mentioned were killed.   On March 19th the Central Committee of the National Guard at last protested against any participation whatever in this slaughter.   In its declaration, which was published in the official journal of the Commune of March 20th, is the following statement:

"We declare with indignation that the bloody disgrace with which our honour has been besmirched is a shocking infamy.   Never did we decide on an execution, and never has the National Guard taken part in any such crime."

This was a strong denunciation, not only of the accusers but also of those cruel deeds which were ascribed to the National Guard.   In view of the secession of the troops to the people, the Government had only two courses open to pursue—either to make concessions to the enraged masses, to bargain with them, or else to retire in flight.   Thiers would, on no account, engage in discussions, but took a headlong flight with his Government out of Paris, and hurried to gather round him all those troops that, as yet, were untainted with the spirit of mutiny.   He even abandoned the forts round Paris, including the prominent fort of Mont Valarien.   If the Parisians had kept to the heels of Thiers, they would perhaps have succeeded in overcoming the Government.   The troops which were withdrawing from Paris would not have been able to offer the least opposition.   That is what their general later on declared.   Then it would have been possible to introduce a new Government, which, however, would not have been able to carry out a Socialist programme.   For that the conditions were not ripe enough.   But they could have dissolved the

National Guard, and have elected a new one with the following programme, namely, the strengthening of the Republic, self-determination for the various districts, Paris included, and the substitution of militia in place of the standing army. More than this, at that time, the Commune did not demand, and this programme was possible at the time on account of the conditions in France. But Thiers continued to retire. They allowed him to take his troops and to reorganise them in Versailles, to fill them with fresh spirit and to strengthen them. Nobody was more surprised at the retreat of the Ministers than the Parisians themselves. There was no organisation at hand that could take over the guidance of affairs in place of the rulers, who had taken flight. Even on the morning of March 19th Paris was entirely without any Government. Force of circumstances made it necessary for the Central Committee of the National Guard to take their place, and thus was formed a body without a fixed programme and without any clear purpose. They discharged their responsibility, in the first place, by delegating their power to a single individual, Lullier, to whom they confided the supreme command over Paris. He was the most unsuitable man conceivable, a drunkard and one who did not know whether he was '' more of a fool than traitor, or vice versa. This man succeeded within the space of forty-eight hours in making the most terrible blunders possible—blunders that could not be remedied. But this unfortunate choice of Lullier was at bottom merely a sign and indication of the situation at that time.''—(Dubreuilh '' La Commune,'' page 283.)

It was not till April 3rd that it was decided to make an attack on Versailles. But what might have brought success on March 19th was on April 3rd a cause of failure. The expectation that the soldiers would again go over to the Parisians as on March 18th ended in bitter disappointment. The Parisian National Guard

stumbled upon most obstinate and determined opposition, which they could not overcome. From that
moment they were put on the defensive against the
whole of France, and in consequence, from that time
onwards their downfall was certain. And from that
time onwards the Paris rising was exclusively proletarian. Up to that moment many of the supporters of
the bourgeois hesitated as to whether or not they should
go over to the proletariat, but henceforth they let the
proletariat alone go on with the fight.

How very differently things proceeded in the insurrection of March 7th, 1917, in Petersburg, as compared
with that of March 18th, 1871, in Paris! This Russian
insurrection was prepared by the Revolutionary Committee, which organised the working classes and the
soldiers, and urged them to attack the Government,
which at that time was in Petersburg, and had as little
strength behind it as had Thiers in 1871 in Paris.
But it is certain that the immediate occupation of
all posts of power in the capital would not have determined the victory of the Bolsheviks, had not the condition of things in the whole Empire been far more
favourable to them than they were for Paris in 1871.
At the time when Kerensky fled to Gatschina, as
formerly Thiers fled to Versailles, he could not reckon
on a peasantry which would uphold him. The
peasantry, and along with it the armed rising in
Russia, all went to the side of the revolutionaries, who
were in power in the capital. This gave their régime
a force and permanent character, which was denied
the Paris regime. On the other hand, it brought about
an economic reactionary element from which the Paris
Commune was saved. The Paris Dictatorship of the
Proletariat was never founded on Peasants' Councils
as was the case in Russia.

WORKMEN'S COUNCILS AND THE CENTRAL
COMMITTEE.

The Paris Commune and the Soviet Republic were
fundamentally different in their starting point, no less
different also in their organisation and the methods
then employed. It is true that the Paris Commune
had an organisation which might easily be compared to
the Workmen's and Soldiers' Council. Indeed, it was
in a similar position to the Russian Revolution, since
it followed, like the Russian, a despotic regime which
prohibited every kind of open political organisation of
the masses, and also forbade the organisation of Trade
Unions only shortly before its downfall. Just as little
as in the case of the Russian workmen in 1905 and
1907, the French workmen, after September 4th, 1870,
found no strong political and Trade Union organisation
ready to hand, which would have enabled them to make
a united fight. This was one of the reasons, as we have
seen, which led Marx to desire so sincerely that the
workers should, in the first place, utilise the new Republic for their own organisation and instruction, and by
this means make it ready and well equipped to act as
a ruling power, and not waste its strength in little
skirmishes, which even in the most favourable circumstances could never give them any lasting supremacy.
But since they came into power by means of a contest
that was forced upon them, and not by a mere skirmish,
they had to be careful to provide, in the absence of any
political and Trade Union organisation, some substitute
which they found ready to hand.   For the Russian
workmen there was such a substitute to be found in the
organisation of gross industry.
"Modern industry has changed the small workshop
of the patriarchal master of former days into the large
factory of the industrial capitalist. Groups of workmen herder together in a factory become organised like
soldiers. Like all ordinary industrial soldiers they are

placed under the supervision of a thorough-going hierarchy of officers and under officers." (Engels to Marx, " Communist Manifesto.")

" The industrial soldiers " of the factory had only to substitute for the officers and under-officers, placed in command by the capitalists, similar officers of their own choice, and hence organisation in the factory became in reality a close organisation of factory workers. Thus arose the institution of the Workmen's Councils among the proletariat of Russia. As against the organisation of party and Trade Unions of countries more advanced than Russia, these Workmen's Councils do not represent any higher form of proletarian organisation, but merely an emergency measure to supply what was lacking. But Paris workmen had no such measure. Parisian industry was, for the most part, industry for the leisured, and not industry for the masses. Even up to the time of the Second Commune, the " small workshop of the patriarchal master " was paramount, since the great factory of the industrial capitalist was almost entirely lacking, the contrary being the case with the industry of Russia, especially in St. Petersburg. The Russian Empire shows its economic backwardness in its lack of industry, and in the small number of industrial workers as against the peasantry. Whatever there is, however, of capitalist industry bears the stamp of modern manufacture on a large scale. The Parisian workmen had to furnish some other substitute for the political and economic organisation of the masses, which at that time was lacking, and this substitute was found in the National Guard. The Revolution of 1789 had as a result the arming of the people everywhere in France, but especially in Paris. This arming served a double purpose. The lower classes, the proletariat and the small middle class took to arms, and organised themselves for insurrection. The Revolution had not brought them what they wanted, and could not bring it them, as the result of the conditions then prevailing.

Hence their persistent impulse, by means of an armed rising, to push the Revolution still further forward. The situation was quite different for the bourgeoisie, the capitalists and the well-to-do middle classes, and the intellectuals who were in quite comfortable circumstances. The Revolution of 1789 brought them exactly what they wanted. They armed and organised themselves in order to defend that which they had won, and they fought on two sides—against the reactionary powers, which strove to restore the ancient feudal absolutism, and also against the lower strata of the people, who were impatiently pursuing their object and pressing forward. Their armed organisation was that of the National Guard. The bourgeoisie remained the victor in the revolutionary struggle, and along with the bourgeoisie the National Guard was established as an institution for the protection of the propertied classes, who themselves nominated their officers and who possessed a certain degree of independence, as against the Government.

The height of importance was attained by the National Guard in the July monarchy, 1830 to 1848. Nevertheless, it could not save that monarchy, and proved itself in 1848 to be very unreliable. Napoleon III., after his *coup d'état*, took from the National Guard its independence, namely, the right to elect its own officers, but he dared not dissolve it completely. Then came the war of 1870 and the speedy defeat. Once again the Fatherland was in danger, and once again the spirits of 1913 were incited to continue the traditions of the victorious fight against Europe, by means of the " levée en masse," through the armed rising of the whole people. Under pressure of this situation, the legislative body in Paris on August 11th proclaimed a law, on the proposal of Jules Favres, that the National Guard, from being a citizen Guard, should be converted into a universal Guard for the whole nation. To the sixty old battalions of the National

Guard, which were drawn from the propertied classes, were attached two hundred new battalions from the poorer classes, who even had the privilege of nominating their own officers. In this way the new battalions of the National Guard of Paris became in reality the organisation of the proletariat. The whole law over the extension of the National Guard was really due to sudden fright rather than to mature reflection. The fathers feared their children, so they decided to do all in their power to prevent these children from gaining strength. But they could not hinder the Paris proletariat from arming itself; the military authorities of Paris, however, under the command of Trocus, omitted everything which could have helped towards the National Guard's developing into troops of any use. In this way they betrayed their Fatherland, but they feared the Paris workmen more than the soldiers of Wilhelm. In Paris, at the beginning of the siege, one hundred thousand troops were to be found, and in addition a hundred thousand Guards. If one assumes that, of the more than three hundred thousand National Guards, two hundred thousand were fit for active service, that makes altogether an army of four hundred thousand men, to which the Germans, when they were outside Paris, could not have opposed more than half the number, which, moreover, were scattered over a very wide area. But from August onwards the National Guard was given ample time to get into shape. As a consequence, the authorities in Paris had a large majority at their disposal to oppose the Germans. If they should succeed in breaking through at any point the iron ring that enclosed Paris, the outlook for the German army of ever winning the war was extremely small. But that would have been possible only if the National Guard could become militarily organised at once. Before this eventuality they shrank. They preferred to lose the war, and to

hand over Alsace-Lorraine to the enemy.   That is
what the Parisians felt, and hence their fury against
those rulers who had betrayed France.   When Paris
had capitulated, and the whole Assembly had been
elected, and when the hatred of this latter body against
the Republic and the capital had come to light in the
most provocative way, the Parisians realised that they
were involved in a serious conflict.   The only power
on which they could rely was the National Guard.
The Revolutionary battalions had already, during the
siege, kept in close contact with one another.   They
now joined into a federation.   Hence they were called
the Federalists.   It was on February 15th that the
delegates of the revolutionary battalions first met
together, in order to discuss the federation.   They
appointed a commission to draw up the Statutes, which
were then laid before the new Assembly on February
24th; but the Assembly was at that time too excited to
deliberate, because a German invasion was feared.
They broke up the meeting, in order to take part in a
revolutionary demonstration on the Place de la
Bastille.   During the following days, a provisional
Central Committee of the National Guard came into
being; which was in the highest degree necessary, in
view of the imminent incursion of the Germans, and
in order to guard against panic.   It was not until
March 3rd that the delegates' Assembly came to anything like a definite organisation.   It was decided
that a Central Committee of the National Guard should
be appointed, consisting of three delegates for each
of the twenty districts (arondissements) of Paris.
Two of the three were elected by the Council of the
Legion, and the third by the Chief of the Battalion
of the Legion.   On March 15th the men chosen as the
definite Central Committee met together, and so dissolved the Provisional Committee, which had functioned hitherto.   One might regard this Central Committee, since it was elected from among the National

Guard, as a Soldiers' Council; but it was chosen from among the proletariat and from the National Guard, who stood in close relation with the proletariat, since the battalion of the leisured classes took no part in these deliberations.   According to the information received by the Central Committee, this latter had supporting it, on March 18th, 215 of the 260 battalions of the Paris National Guard.   So far, therefore, it was a kind of Workmen's Council.   One can therefore quite well compare it with the Central Committee of Workmen's and Soldiers' Councils.   Nevertheless, the Paris Commune was by no means a Soviet Republic. When on March 18th the Government took to flight, there was none to occupy public office.   This very naturally fell to the Central Committee, for it was the only organisation in Paris that was held in universal esteem, although all its members were wholly unknown people.   On March 10th they met together, in order to deliberate what was to be done.   As is so often the case, they formulated the problem on this occasion as an " either, or " whereas a " both, and " would have been more to the point.   Thus the Socialists repeatedly discussed the question whether there should be reform or revolution, instead of saying that the striving for reform and the struggle for revolution should be so conducted, that neither one of these movements should exclude the other, but rather support it.

On March 19th some members of the Central Committee demanded that a march should be made against Versailles.   Others wanted to appeal to the electors then and there, and again, others wanted first of all to take revolutionary measures.   As if each one of these steps was not equally necessary, and as if any of them could exclude the other!   The Central Committee decided, in the first place, to take only one of these steps, and one that seemed to be the most imperative.   It wished to show that behind the Paris rising the majority of the electors was to be found, and it wished in this way to give the insurrection the greatest moral support. That was perfectly right; only it would have been more advantageous to strengthen, by means of revolutionary power, the moral authority of the General Election as against the enemy, who himself was undoubtedly endeavouring to get the support of the army. The immediate election of a communal administration for Paris, based on universal suffrage, which the Empire had hitherto withheld from the Parisians, was certainly inevitable. Immediately after the downfall of the Empire in September, 1870, the Paris workmen had obtained from the new provisional Government the assurance that the election of a commune would soon be undertaken. The failure to fulfil this promise contributed not a little to the disorders that arose during the siege. The insurrections of October 31st and of January 22nd took place amid the cries of "Long live the Commune." Hence it was necessary to make at once a complete list of the electors for the Commune. It was arranged first for the 22nd, and then for the 26th of March. The Central Committee regarded itself merely as a temporary body to hold places in reserve for those who should be elected by universal and equal suffrage. In the *Journal Officiel de la République Française de la Commune* of March 20th, the following announcement was made to the citizens of Paris:

"In three days you will be called upon, in perfect freedom, to elect members for district representation of Paris. Those who have seized power as the result of necessity will then hand over their provisional authority into the hands of the elected of the people."

But they did not stick to their promise. After the Commune had been constituted the Central Committee delegated its power to that body on March 28th. It even went so far as to give signs that it would dissolve completely; but the Commune did not insist on this, and so this Central Committee continued to function under the Commune as a part of the military machinery. This did not serve to facilitate the carrying on of business, nor the conduct of war. But the Central Committee never attempted to upset the principle that the supreme power belonged to those elected by universal suffrage. This Central Committee never claimed that all power should fall to the Workmen's and Soldiers' Councils, that is, in the present case, to the Central Committee of the workmen's battalions. In this point also, therefore, the Paris Commune was the exact contrary to the Russian Republic, and yet Freiderich Engels wrote on March 18th, 1891, on the twentieth anniversary of the Paris Commune: "Gentlemen, do you want to know what the dictatorship of the proletariat looks like? Look at the Paris Commune. That was the dictatorship of the proletariat." We see that Marx and Engels, under the title of dictatorship, in no way understood the withholding of universal and equal suffrage, or the suppression of democracy.

The Jacobins in the Commune.

At the election on March 26, ninety members of the Commune were elected. These included fifteen Government supporters, and six citizen radicals who were in opposition to the Government, but who nevertheless condemned the insurrection. A Soviet Republic would never have allowed such elements of the counter-revolutionaries to appear as candidates, let alone to be elected as members. The Commune, out of its respect for democracy, never hindered its civil opponents from election. If their activity in the Commune came to a sudden end, this was their own fault. The company in which they found themselves was not to their liking, and they very soon took their departure. Some, indeed, retired before the election candidates met together, and others, a few days after the Commune was established. These resignations, as well as certain mandates, made a re-election imperative, and this took place on April 16th. The great majority of the members of the Commune were on the side of the insurrection. Moreover, among the revolutionary members of the Commune, not all were Socialists. The majority consisted simply of revolutionaries. Most of them were guided by the principles laid down in 1793, and by the traditions of the Jacobins. Some had already shown their allegiance in 1848 to the "Mountain," for instance, Delescluse and Pyat, and not a few were forced out of their private professional life as the result of their political struggle, and became conspirators and revolutionaries by profession. The older members among them lived according to the traditions of the past, and had no real interest for new developments and conceptions.

"The others, that is the younger ones, were to a large extent men who resorted to force without any sound foundation. They were often merely heroes in word, and were now playing with the insurrection just as, a few months before, they had played with wars —men who talked a great deal and contented themselves with mere talking. Their revolutionary ideas were confined to mere externalities. They were superficial, and even the very best of them were actuated by feeling rather than by reason." This is the criticism of these men given by that great revolutionary, Dubreuilh. ("La Commune," page 332.)

Most of them understood nothing about Socialism. Not a few of them were directly against it, especially Delescluse. One could not call them bourgeoise politicians in the sense that they at all represented the interests of the propertied classes. On the contrary they stood side by side with the lower classes and fought for them as much as the people of the "Mountain" of 1793 had done. But just like these latter,

they could not escape from the questions of property
and privilege belonging to the bourgeois classes, and for
this reason they may be said to have formed a bourgeois element. This applies to the majority of the
revolutionaries in the Commune. Only a few of them
belonged to the working classes. Among them were
to be found ordinary officials, apothecaries, investors,
lawyers, and, above all, journalists. Different from the
Jacobins were the Blanquistes, seven in number,
among them Blanqui himself, who, however, could not
take his seat. It shows how little the Blanquistes
expected the insurrection of March 18th, for Blanqui,
shortly before the outbreak, in order to recuperate his
health, had left Paris. On March 17th he was arrested
in Figeac (Department Lot). Blanqui agreed with the
Jacobins on one point, namely, in their endeavour, by
means of an insurrection on the part of the lower classes
in Paris, to govern Paris; and through Paris, by means
of a regime of force, the whole of France. But they
went further than the Jacobins, since they recognised
that this method of government would not suffice to
liberate the exploited, unless that government could
be used to create a new social order. In other words
they were Socialists. Yet in their case it was always
the political rather than the economic interest that
weighed most with them. They did not study economic
life, nor did they endeavour to gain any systematic
economic knowledge. They betrayed this characteristic
by frequently excusing ignorance, saying that they
wished to be entirely untrammelled by dogma. They
did not want to be "bewildered" by prejudices and
"academic discussion." When the proletariat came
into power, they said, it would very soon know what it
had to do. Their chief concern was to give the proletariat this power, and they regarded the insurrection,
which was being prepared, as a means towards this
end.

They were unfortunate, however, since the insurrections which they carefully prepared always came to grief, and the one that was successful found them unprepared. Moreover, the Blanquiste teaching made no great claims on the intelligence, but contented itself with immediate action. Indeed, this teaching had enormous attraction for men of action. In spite of this fact, however, it found more acceptance among the intellectuals, especially students, than among the workmen.

The following is a tabulation of the elements which constituted the Blanquiste Party at that time. On November 17th, 1866, a secret meeting of the Blanquiste group was surprised by the police in a Paris café and the members were arrested. There were forty-one, and each one's occupation was given. These included fourteen artisans, four shop assistants, thirteen students, six journalists, one lawyer, one foreman, one landowner, and one independent merchant. The number of students would have been far greater, only on November 7th the holidays were not yet at an end, and so many students were absent from Paris.

This meeting throws a light upon Blanquism, not only on the manner of its constitution but also on its aims. In September, 1866, the International Congress met in Geneva, and the Blanquistes were invited to attend. Blanqui refused, but two of the chosen delegates, namely, the lawyer Protot and the employee Humbert, nevertheless went. In consequence there was great excitement in the Blanquiste camp; for, according to its traditions, the dictatorship belonged, not only to the proletariat, but also to the leader of their party. Both kinds of dictatorship were closely connected. For the first time since the existence of the Blanquiste organisation an order from the head of the party had been disobeyed. Up to that time they had followed in blind obedience, and even later they adhered to this principle. A meeting was held on

November 7th in order to bring Protot to judgment; but this meeting was dissolved before any conclusion was reached. A few were able to take to flight, among them Protot himself. The others, as we have said, were arrested. (Charles Da Costa, " Les Blanquistes," Paris, 1912, pages 17-22).

Among the Blanquistes of the Commune were found the lawyer Protot again, and also two of the members who were arrested on November 7th. They were the lawyer Tridon and the student Raoul Rigault. Among the others elected were Blanqui, a lawyer and a doctor (who had studied both faculties), Eudes, an apothecary, and Ferré, an accountant. In the whole Blanquiste faction was found only one single working man, the coppersmith Chardon. Of the elected members of the International who were found in the Commune two had relations with the Blanquistes, namely, a smith, Duval, and the student Vaillant. We see how much the intellectuals preponderated amongst them. Even within the Commune itself, the Jacobins, like the Blanquistes, troubled little about economic questions. The war against Versailles, the policing of Paris, and the struggle against the Church—these were the questions to which they devoted their energies. This last struggle also, like the military struggle against Versailles and the police struggle against the Versailles associates in Paris, was carried out by means of force, and by an attack on persons and externalities.

THE INTERNATIONAL AND THE COMMUNE.

The third of the groups in the Commune was formed by members of the International, seventeen in number, almost exclusively Proudhonistes. Proudhonism was in sharp contrast to Blanquism and Jacobinism. The Regiment of Terror of 1793 was for Proudhonism something to be avoided, not to be imitated. It saw very clearly the weaknesses of this regiment and the unavoidability of its failure. It realised that the mere acquirement of political power on the part of the proletariat could alter nothing in its social position, and that it could not abolish the system of exploitation from which the proletariat suffered. It realised further that the change could be reached, not by political disturbances but only through an economic reorganisation. This, therefore, made the Proudhonistes suspicious of the Blanquiste methods, suspicious of the insurrection and of Terrorism, and none the less opposed to democracy. In the February Revolution of 1848 the Parisian Proletariat had conquered the democracy; but what had it gained by its action? A growing mistrust of the proletarian struggle for political freedom, and of the participation of the proletariat in matters of policy animated the Proudhonistes.

To-day similar ideas have arisen, and are offered as the latest products of Socialistic thought, as the product of experience, which Marx neither knew nor could know of. These are merely variations of ideas that are over half a century old, but they have not for that reason become more correct. Proudhonism showed how a policy for the liberation of the proletariat, undertaken by means of an economic transformation alone, is doomed to failure. To-day we preach about the powerlessness of democracy to free the proletariat, so long as this proletariat is held bound in the chains of capitalism. But if economic liberation must precede the political, then, logically, every kind of political activity on the part of the proletariat is equally useless, of whatever kind it may be. Whereas the Blanquistes devoted their attention exclusively to the political struggle against the existing powers of State, Proudhonism, equally exclusively, sought means to give the proletariat economic freedom, without any

assistance from the State. As a consequence, the
Blanquistes reproached the Proudhonistes for dis-
couraging the working classes in their struggle against
the Second Empire, under which they lay bleeding. Even
Marx accused Proudhon, saying that '' he coquetted
with Louis Bonaparte and endeavoured to justify him
in the eyes of the French working-men.''   (In his
article of January, 1865, which appeared in the
German edition of ''Misery of Philosophy,'' second
edition, page 32.)   On the other hand, the
Proudhonistes were conscious of the class antagonism
between the proletariat and the bourgeois, for the
good reason that, with the Proudhonistes, the economic
question was of first importance.   They realised,
further, that the proletariat would have to trust to its
own strength to gain its freedom.   They realised this
far more than the Blanquistes; for these latter were
to a large extent a student party, whereas the
Proudhonistes formed the real Labour Party in France
under the Second Empire.

When in the 'sixties the Labour Movement everywhere awoke from the death-sleep into which it fell, as
a result of the reaction after 1848, and at the time when
the International of the working party was being
formed, it was the Proudhonistes in France who joined
up with them. This was reason enough for Blanqui
to forbid his followers to attach themselves also. In
the International, however, they learnt to know of a
new order of theory and practice, which made them
turn away all the more from one-sided Proudhonism.
For just at the time of the foundation of the International Labour League, their leader, Proudhon, died
on January 19th, 1865, and in France a new condition
arose for the continuation of the class struggle.
Proudhon wished to inaugurate a purely labour movement without politics, but that was possible only by
renouncing all attempts at a struggle that would
involve their coming into conflict with State authority.

Quite peaceful means were to be employed to free the working classes, namely, guilds, banks of exchange, a mutual system of insurance. These ideas were possible in Paris where industry, as has been shown before, had very little of the character of manufacture on a large scale, and where the exploiting capitalist appeared to the workman much more as the monied capitalist, taking all the profits. than as a real industrial contractor.

In the International the French Proudhonistes learnt something of English industrial capitalism, and of a Labour Movement corresponding to this capitalism, which laid most emphasis, in economic matters, on the importance of the organisation of their struggle, on Trade Unions and strikes, with which the Proudhonist would have nothing to do. Over and above this system of practice, there arose a theory which shed the clearest light upon the laws underlying modern society and social life, a theory which was still unknown to the majority of the International, and was not rightly understood even by those who knew. The creator of this theory, however, by his immense superiority, inspired the International in all its activity with his spirit and ideas. In Marx's theory, the one-sidedness of Proudhonism and of Blanquism also was overcome. Like the Proudhonistes, Marx recognised that the economic relations were of the first importance, and that without some alteration of these relations no political change of whatever kind could possibly emancipate the proletariat. But, none the less, he recognised that the possession of State power and authority was absolutely necessary in order to break the domination of capital, and in order to carry out the emancipation of the proletariat by economic changes. The fundamental importance of the economic factor received at the hands of Marx an utterly different character from that given by Proudhon. Economics in the eyes of Marx made poli tics not superfluous, but necessary. The character and outcome of political struggle and its very effect depended, to a large extent, on the economic question. But he realised that economic conditions themselves form a steadily progressing process, which makes a political result possible to-day and inevitable to-morrow, whereas yesterday it seemed impossible. The relation between economics and politics consisted for him in studying the economic conditions and tendencies, and in attempting to make political aims and methods fit in with them. The Blanquistes and Proudhonistes, on the other hand, entirely neglected the historical aspect. Their chief endeavour was not at any given moment to find out what was possible and necessary from an economic point of view, but to find the means which, under all conditions and in all historical and economic circumstances, should give the desired result. If the Socialists have found the right means, they are then in a position to carry out their Socialism exactly as they wish. It was believed that these ideas had been superseded by Marxism, but we find them still in existence even to-day. Once again we find men in Moscow and Budapest who, instead of asking what policy is possible and necessary in the present economic conditions, are proceeding from the standpoint that, since Socialism is desired by the Proletariat, the Socialists have a duty to carry out their Socialism, wherever they have the power to do so. Their duty consists not in examining whether, and how far, this scheme is possible, but in discovering where the Philosopher's stone is to be found, that universal remedy which Socialism, in all circumstances and in all conditions, undertakes to provide. And people of the present day believe that this problem has been solved by the proclamation of the dictatorship on the basis of the Council system. In the Second French Empire the Blanquistes thought to discover the

Philosopher's stone in a revolt, the Proudhonistes, in the banks of exchange.

Even at the present day Marx has been little understood. He demanded far too great mental energy and far too great subordination of personal desires and needs. But, in a general way, all the aims, ways, and means adopted by him, as well as by Engels, were successful, because the logic of things was on their side. In consequence, the Marxist ideas gradually ousted the Proudhonist ideas from the French Internationalists. As soon as the Labour movement again came to life in France, Trade Unions and strikes were inevitable. The Empire endeavoured to lead the movement on legal and non-political lines, and sanctioned the formation, in 1864, of Trade Unions, as well as the carrying out of strikes—in the very year in which the International was founded. The members of this International, including the Proudhonistes, not only were forced to take part in this spontaneous Labour movement, but circumstances forced them, as the best representatives of the economic interests of the Labour classes, to come to the head of the organisation and the movement. It was inevitable that they should thus come into conflict with the State authority, and in this way they were drawn into the political struggle, into the struggle against the Empire. Under these circumstances the ideas of the French Internationalists, which at the start had been Proudhonist in character, became more and more Marxist in colour. Yet, at the outbreak of the revolt of the Commune, not one of them could be described as a Marxist. They had lost their old Proudhonist foundation, but had not yet gained new ground. Their ideas were still lacking in clearness. Nevertheless they were the members of the Commune who took the most trouble to examine economic life, and who best understood the vital needs of the time. They formed the real Labour representatives in the Commune. Lissagaray says about them:—

" People have said that the Commune was a Government of the working classes. That is a great mistake. The working classes took part in the struggle, in the administration, and their breath alone made the movement great; but they were very little engaged in actual government. The election of March 26th gave the workers only 25 votes as against 70, which went to the revolutionaries." (" History of the Commune," second edition, page 145.)

But of these 25, the majority, 13, belonging to the International, had all told only 17 representatives in the Commune. Only four of the International were not Labour members and of these one of them, the student, Vaillant, had leanings towards the Blanquistes. Out of the 13 members of the Labour group among the Internationals we find the most important men in the Commune, namely the bookbinder, Varlin, the carpenter, Theiss, the painter, Malon, and the jeweller, Frankel. In accordance with their Party standpoint they left all direct action, the conduct of the war, and the organisation of the police, to the Jacobins and Blanquistes, and turned their attention to the question of peace, to the administration of the districts, and to economic changes. Only one of them showed any warlike spirit, namely, the metal worker, Duval, and he was inclined, as we know, like Vaillant, to Blanquism. He was one of those in the Commune who, at the outbreak of April 3rd, was captured and shot by order of General Vinoy. Thus he was one of the first martyrs of the Commune.

His comrades in the International confined their attention almost entirely to the economic problems, and they did remarkably good work, namely, in administration. For instance, Theiss in postal arrangements, Varlin and Avrial in other important positions of command, in spite of the enormous difficulties, which arose from the fact that the higher officials having fled from Paris, or at least from their positions, the working classes had suddenly to take over and carry on work to which they were wholly strangers. Along with the Internationalists of the Commune there were other members of the Paris International who were successful in their labours, for instance, the bronze worker, Camelinat, who, in the month of April, took over the coinage, and in a very few weeks made vast improvements, which, after the fall of the Commune, were still maintained. Then there was Bastelica who undertook the direction of customs, and Combault, Director of Indirect Taxation. Both were workmen.

One of the first actions on the part of the Commune consisted in handing over the separate districts of the Executive, not to individual ministers but to special commissions. The Commission for Labour, Industry and Exchange, also the Commission representing the Socialist side of the Commune consisted of the Internationalists Malin, Theiss, Dupont (basket maker), and Avrial (mechanic), Gerardin and one single Jacobin, whose occupation I could not find. Of the five members of the Commission for Finance, three belonged to the International, the painter, Victor Clément Varlin. and the rather wealthy philanthropist, Beslay, one of the few bourgeois in the International. Besides these men there were the Jacobin, Regère, a veterinary surgeon, but an old fighter against the Empire, as well as the cashier, Jourdes, who had no particular tendencies, and who was the real head of finance, through whose hands millions of francs had to pass, while his wife continued to carry on the family washing in the Seine, he himself never dining at a higher cost than 1.60 fr. In both the Commissions for labour and finance utterly different methods were employed from those in the Commissions for the army and police. The contrast in these methods has been very well characterised by Mendlessohn, in his appendix to Lissagaray's, " History of the Commune " (second German edition).

" The war administration in the Commune had very little satisfactory means to hand. Here we find incapacity, ignorance, vanity, absence of all feeling for responsibility, etc. Here we find the reflection of all the unfortunate disorganisation of the conditions under which the Socialist movement had to suffer during the Empire, and we need only go from the Place Vendôme to the Prefecture of Police, in order to find the second reflection of these conditions.

" We certainly find a peaceful change from the noisy self-importance of the new Hebertists, who formed the general staff of police at the time, when we pass over to the Ministry of Labour and the Ministry of Exchange. The name itself shows the influence of the Proudhonist doctrine. Apart from this, however, the conscientious and modest members of the International were so occupied in their labour, that they put aside all that was impossible and fantastic. Regarding themselves as a committee of the working-classes, they did not look for signs of their power in orders and badges. They formed a commission out of the members of the Trade Unions and Labour Commissions. As a result, this Ministry so carried on its work, that one can say it did what it could according to the conditions then prevailing, and never undertook anything that it could not carry out."

In this Ministry the Socialists stood well concentrated. It was Marxist in character. It represented the actual revolutionary elements in the Commune, and yet it showed a measure of caution, which was perfectly amazing. The reason for this caution, which was also noticeable in the Ministry of Finance, was given by Jourde on the occasion of a debate on pawnbrokers' shops. It was ordered that pledged clothes, household furniture and utensils up to twenty francs in value should be returned to their original owners

without payment from May 12th onwards. The State undertook the compensation. In the course of this debate Avrial proposed that in the place of these pawn-brokers' shops a better kind of Labour institute should be established, whereupon Jourde replied:
" They say form an institute. But that is all very well. We must first have time in order to study the question before we do anything. If Avrial was told to manufacture cannons he would demand more time. I demand that also." (Sitting of May 6th, *Officiel Journal* of May 7th, page 493.)

The Commune found no time to do anything on a large scale on the social question, and the best people among them would not undertake anything, without thoroughly studying the question first. Most of their social measures would to-day seem trivial. For instance, the suspension of night labour among the bakers, and the prohibition of fines in business houses. The most important conclusion never got beyond mere examination. During the siege and after March 18th there was a large number of factories in Paris closed down by their owners, who fled and escaped. On the proposal of Avrial an inquiry into this very serious question for the working classes was made, and the conclusion ran as follows:

" In consideration of the fact that numerous factories have been closed down by those who hitherto ran them, in order that the owners might avoid their civil duties, and without taking into consideration the interests of the workmen; further, in consideration of the fact that, through this cowardly flight from their positions, much important labour for the communal life has been interrupted, and that the working ·nan is thus endangered, the Commune of Paris makes the following declaration:

" The Trade Unions of the workmen shall be called together, in order to form commissions of inquiry with the following object in view:

" (1) To gather statistics of the businesses thus closed down, as well as an exact description of the state in which they are at present, as well as of the machinery contained therein:

" (2) To provide a report as to the practical measures to be taken in order to put these factories into working order, not through those who have deserted them, but through associations of workmen who were employed in them;

" (3) To form a scheme of action for these associations;

" (4) To set up a court of arbitration, which shall settle under what conditions these factories shall be definitely handed over to the possession of these Labour associations, when the owners who have fled shall return to Paris; and further, to decide on the compensation that these associations shall make to the original owners. This Commission of Inquiry must lay its report before the Commune Commission for Labour and Exchange. Furthermore, and in the shortest possible time, a synopsis of this decree, which shall serve the interests of the Commune and of the workmen, is to be laid before the Commune."

This Order is dated April 16th and the *Journal Officiel*, April 17th.

This Commission of Inquiry met together on May 10th and 19th. Soon after that came the defeat of the Commune. That socialising Commission therefore came to no practical result. Nevertheless, its formation was of importance, for it pointed the way which the Socialists of the Commune would have been forced to go, if the proletariat regime had been of longer duration. There could be no question of a complete socialising or of an immediate elimination of the whole system of capitalistic enterprise. On the contrary, these very men were reproached for abandoning their factories in such a cowardly manner, and for leaving the working man without employment. At the same time, however, the contrary reproof was hurled at them.

The Central Committee of the twenty arondisse-ments (districts) (not to be confused with that of the National Guard, which had been formed during the Siege), complained that the employers had kept the workmen in the factories, and in this way prevented them from fulfilling their duty as members of the National Guard. Only those concerns which had been abandoned by their owners were to be socialised, in the first place, according to the plan of the Commune; and only these after very careful and exact consider-ation. Another step in the direction of socialisation was planned in connection with supplies for army uniforms and ammunition. These supplies were, as far as possible, to be made through the workmen's associations on the basis of Treaties of Supplies, which were to be drawn up by the Director, in common with the Guards and the Minister of Labour. There is to hand a scheme of Labour Order, which was submitted by the workers to the Commune, and which was concerned with the factories employed in repairing arms, and demanded a fixed ten-hours day. This Order, which contains some twenty-two para-graphs, was printed in the *Journal Officiel de la Commune* on May 21st (pages 628-629). It shows very well the socialising tendencies of the Socialist workers of the Commune. In accordance with this Order, the workers elected their own representatives of work-shops in the Commune, their own superintendent, as well as their foremen. A Management Council was formed consisting of the above officials, to which a workman from each worker's bench was allowed to come. On the part of the Commune a Supervisory Council was to be formed, which should be duly informed of all that was done, and which had free access to inspect the books and ledgers. The workmen showed themselves to be very anxious to uphold the interests of the Commune. In Article 15 the scheduled time was fixed at ten hours per day, and not at eight, which the International Congress of Geneva in 1866 had demanded. In special cases of urgency overtime was permitted, if the Management Council agreed. For any overtime no increased pay was granted. Apart from this, the wages at that time were very low. The Director received 250 francs a month, the manager 210, the foreman 70 cents. an hour. For the ordinary worker there was no minimum wage fixed, but a maximum wage. He could not receive more than 60 cents. an hour. Interesting also is the declaration contained in Article 16, which ordains that there should always be a night watchman in the workshops in case of weapons being needed. Every workman was bound to take his turn at night duty. The conclusion ran as follows:

" As under the present circumstances it is absolutely necessary to be as economical as possible with every farthing of the Commune, the night watchman will not be paid." (*Journal Officiel*, page 629.)

Truly these workmen did not regard the time of their " dictatorship " as an opportune moment for demanding an increase of wages. The great and general cause for good, in their estimation, had a higher claim than their own personal interests.

The Socialism of the Commune.

In spite of his volcanic temperament, Marx did not find anything in these precautionary measures to which he could not agree. He said in his " Civil War in France," page 53:

" The great social measure adopted by the Commune was one for the existence of the working element. This special measure could only point the way in which a government of the people, through the people, could function."

After Marx had so described the dictatorship of the proletariat as the government of the people through the people, in other words, as democracy, he continues, and praises the financial measures adopted by the Commune as "excellent both in their *wisdom* and *moderation*" (page 54).

Shortly before, Marx shows in the same work the principles on which a period of transition from capitalism to Socialism must proceed:—

"The working classes did not demand any miracle from the Commune. It had no ready-made Utopias to introduce, as a result of popular decision. It knew that, in order to obtain its own freedom, and to fashion along with that some better standard of living, which the present state of society had made impossible through the economic complications then existing, the working class would have to go through a long process of preparation, and sustain many fights before men, as well as circumstances, could be completely transformed. It had no ideals to realise. It had merely to give the elements of the new society freedom to expand, the elements which were already latent in the crumbling bourgeois society" (page 50).

From the sentence, "the working class had no ideals to realise," it has been concluded that Marx contributed to the Social movement no set aim and no definite programme. But this is disproved by the fact that he himself drew up the Socialistic programmes from "The Communist Manifesto" of 1847 onwards to the time of the programme of the French Labour Party, which he finished in 1880 with the collaboration of Guesde and Lafargue. In the above-cited paragraph he already gives the aims of the Social movement, namely, emancipation of the working class by means of victory and progressive class war, and the creation of a better standard of living, which would follow from the coming into power of the working class, and which would be based on the results of modern science.

It might be urged against Marx that these aims were nothing else but ideals, and therefore that the working class had still ideals to realise, but among the ideals which were not realisable Marx clearly understands all transcendental ideas, such as lie beyond the spheres of time and place, such, for instance, as the ideas of eternal justice and freedom. The aims of the workers' movement were provided by the economic development that was then in progress. The special forms of their realisation are in a continuous state of development, and are indeed dependent on time and space. Socialism is for him no ready-made Utopia, but a process which promises a lengthy development of economic relations and also of the working class itself, a development which should not come to an end after a political victory, but which could only continue by setting at liberty " the elements of the new society."

Already two decades before Marx had prescribed a lengthy preparation on the part of the working class, and the knowledge of the actual state of affairs as conditions necessary for the social revolution. After the breaking up of the Revolution of 1848, he recognised, as a result of his study of the economic conditions, that the Revolution for the time being had come to an end. This brought him into conflict with many of his comrades, who saw in this mere treachery towards the Revolution. The masses had need of a revolution, and they had the will for it; and therefore it was inevitable, so they said. But Marx replied in September, 1850, in the following words:—

" In place of a critical examination the minority (the League of the Communists) sets up the dogmatic; instead of the materialistic conception of things, the idealistic. Instead of the actual condition of things being the driving force of the Revolution, they seek

for that driving force in mere will; whereas we say to
the workmen, ' you have to go through twenty or fifty
years of civil wars and struggles, not only to change
conditions but also to change yourselves, and to make
yourselves capable of political government.' You say
to the workmen, on the contrary, ' we must at once
seize power or we might as well lie down and sleep.'
Whereas we point out, specially to the German
workers, the undeveloped state of the German proletariat, you flatter in the crudest manner possible their
national feelings and the class prejudice of the German
artisan, which is naturally much more popular.

" Just as the democrats have converted the word
' people ' into something almost sacred, you have
done the same with the word ' proletariat.' Like
the democrats you substitute the word ' revolution '
for ' revolutionary development.' " Marx: (" Dis
closures in connection with the Communist Congress in
Cologne," new issue, 1885).

When Marx protested against the idea that mere
will should be made the driving force of the Revolution,
he did not mean to say, of course, that the will had
nothing to do with the matter. Without will-power no
conscious ˉaction is possible. Without the *will*, no
revolution is possible, indeed no history. The first
condition of every social movement lies in the strong
will, which social endeavour engenders, and which
arises from a deeply felt need. But with the *will
alone* nothing can be achieved   If the movement is
to have any success, there must be something
more than the *mere will* and *mere need*. I may have
the *will* to live for ever, and this *will* may be unusually
strong in me, nevertheless it cannot preserve me
from death. If then the movement is to have success,
the will must confine itself to what is possible, and the
need must find the means to secure its own satisfaction. Moreover, those who *will* to do anything must
possess the power to overcome any opposition that

may arise.   It is the purpose of discussion to distinguish, as a result of the examination of actual conditions, the possible from the impossible, and to show the mutual relation of strength.   In this way the latent powers in humanity can be concentrated on what is practicable at the time.   In this way all waste of energy may be avoided, and the existing power may be turned to better use, and operate more intensively.

This discernment in social matters is, however, by no means easy to obtain; for the economic foundations of society are in a state of continuous development and change, and, in addition, social needs change also, as well as the means by which these needs shall be satisfied, and the forces which shall accomplish what is practically possible.   Moreover, society becomes more complicated, wider in its embrace, and ever more difficult to penetrate.   Certainly human intelligence, it is true, increases, and the methods of knowledge improve, but the human mind is not always fashioned to recognise actual relations as they are.   It always tries to satisfy the needs of the time.   But wherever the actual condition of things renders the satisfaction of these needs impossible, the human mind is only too inclined, from sheer imagination, to read into these conditions a very friendly aspect in accordance with what it desires.   Man does not wish to die, but knowledge of actual conditions tells him that he must die.   Yet human penetration has managed to discover in these very conditions some sign that we continue in existence after death.   The proletariat of the Roman Empire lived in wretched poverty.   Nevertheless they felt most strongly the need for a joyous life of pleasure without work; but actual conditions excluded such a life from the bounds of possibility.   Despite all, their human instincts promised them such a life in the direction in which they thought they were going.

The idea of the deity was the means to make the weak strong, and the impossible possible.   It was to

raise the small, ill-treated Jewish people to be lords of
the earth. It would give the indignant band of defenceless peasants, at the time of the Reformation, the
victory over the well-equipped and well-disciplined
armies of the potentates of that time. In the nineteenth century the proletariat discontinued to believe
in a deity that would thus come to the rescue; but
the picture of the great French Revolution, in which
at certain times the proletariat of Paris was able to
challenge the whole of Europe, caused a new belief in
miracles to arise, which made them believe in the
wondrous powers of the Revolution and the revolutionary proletariat. They needed merely to *will* in
order to achieve *what* they willed. If nothing came of
it, that was due merely to the fact that they had not
willed. As against this idealistic conception, Marx
championed the materialistic view, which insisted that
the actual conditions of things should always be taken
into account. Certainly these conditions made the
emancipation of the working classes and a higher
standard of living one of its aims which '' the present
state of society, as the result of its development,
absolutely possesses.'' These aims were not, however, to be immediately achieved, like some '' ready
made Utopia.'' They did not form a complete scheme
applicable to all times, but engendered merely a new
form of social movement and development.

The working class, therefore, is not always, and in
all circumstances, mature enough to take over control.
It must everywhere go through a period of development, in order to become capable. Furthermore, it
cannot choose the moment when it shall come into
power. If the working class does take over control,
then it must not simply destroy the means of production which it finds in existence. It must rather
seek to carry on what is already existent, to develop
it further in accordance with the needs of the
proletariat, and to''liberate the elements of the new

society," all which in different circumstances requires very different treatment. It will thus at any given moment more easily find what is attainable the more clearly it understands the actual conditions and takes them into account.

When, after the downfall of Napoleon, the possibilities of a proletarian Revolution arose, Marx gave it a good deal of serious thought. Certainly the Parisian workers were the most intelligent workers in the world at that time. They were not living in vain in the very heart of the world, in the very home of enlightenment and revolution. Nevertheless, the Empire had denied them a good school-system, freedom of the Press, as well as political, and for a long time also industrial, organisation. Therefore, to make use of the Republic for the better education and organisation of the working classes, to uphold and defend the Republic with every means in power, seemed to Marx to be the most imperative need of the time. There was one circumstance which rendered acquisition of political power by the workers at the time impossible, namely, the fact that the greater part of the country was still agrarian, and the population of Paris itself still largely small bourgeois. Moreover, the world's history does not depend upon our mere will power. It can just as little postpone the coming of revolution as it can hasten it. The rising of the Paris workers and their victory on March 18th were inevitable. From henceforth it was for the people to become clear as to what the actual state of affairs permitted the victorious proletariat to carry out, and to concentrate all their strength upon this design.

Marx did not regard it as the chief duty of the Paris Commune at that time to do away with all capitalistic means of production. He wrote to Kugelmann about this on April 12th, 1871:

" If you will turn up the last chapter of my ' 18th Brumère ' you will find that I proposed, as the next attempt for the French Revolution, to undertake that they should not endeavour to wrest the bureaucratic military machine out of the hands of one man and give it to another, but smash it up completely. This is the necessary condition of every real popular revolution on the Continent. This is also what our heroic comrades in Paris are attempting." (" The New Times," No. 20, 1, page 709.)

There is no word of Socialism in this letter. Marx proclaims that the chief duty of the Commune is to destroy the power then in the hands of the bureaucrats, the militarists. Obviously the proletariat can never come to the head of affairs without striving, along with the changes in the organisation of the State, to realise also the changes in the organisation of the means of production, which should ameliorate its position. If we characterise all such attempts at political power with this end in view as Socialism, then certainly there was Socialism in the Commune, but State Socialism was far removed from what we to-day understand as Socialism. Naturally that was due in part to want of time. The whole rising lasted only a few weeks. For the most part this was due to the fact that this rising was confined to the small industrial elements in Paris. As the result of the existing economic basis, little more could be achieved than the transformation of single workshops into associations of productive workers.

The organisation of a complete branch of industry into a unified system of production and control of its exports, as well as of its raw materals, was hardly possible at that time. If the Commune had been successful, it might have acquired for itself the whole of the State and Government machinery. It might also have introduced nationalisation of railways, perhaps also of mines and ironworks. But all this would not

E

have done away with capitalism, for it was already in operation to a large extent, or at least in preparation, in neighbouring Germany. But under a proletarian and democratic regime it would nevertheless have greatly raised the social position of the working-class. In addition to lack of time and to the economic backwardness of the country, there came a further serious hindrance to "socialisation," namely, the ignorance of the men who were in the Commune. The Jacobins and Blanquistes cared not one farthing for economic matters. The Internationalists, as we have seen, attributed to them the greatest importance; yet just at the time of the Commune they were theoretically untenable. These Internationalists had the intention of abandoning the Proudhonist basis, but they were not prepared to go so far and deliberately put themselves on the side of the Marxists. In the meanwhile, in spite of their fears, Marx agreed with the method of the Commune, namely, first of all to examine the economic question before making any changes, and not to introduce hasty decrees, which would fail of their object, cause confusion, and finally discouragement. Even if this caution arose more from theoretic uncertainty than from theoretic discernment, it agreed with all that Marx, in consequence of his materialistic conception of things, regarded as necessary, namely, that in the Revolution we must be guided not by mere will alone, but by a knowledge of the actual state of affairs. Debreuilh has characterised this feature of the Paris rising extraordinarily well in his "Commune," page 419.

"The policy of methodic expropriation, quite apart from the opposition of the other classes, was impossible, for the very good reason that the day labourers in the mass had no idea of the constitution of society other than the traditional one, and because they had not developed any institutions or trade guilds, which are absolutely necessary to ensure the

normal working of production and exchange after all
capitalistic organisation has been removed.   It is
impossible to improvise a new regime, especially a
Socialistic regime, by means of decrees.   Decrees and
laws should rather make secure the relations already
existing.   If in this matter the Commune had
attempted to act prematurely, probably the sole
result would have been to cause a section of its own
best powers to turn against it, without causing among
the daily workers any appreciable disposition in their
favour.   They could not do otherwise than prepare the
way for a general social provision, under the pretence
of democratising the political machinery then in existence; and that is what they did." (Debreuilh.)

In this way the Marxian idea of the Dictatorship of
the Proletariat was realised on the social plane.   This
Marxian method of socialisation, which was so very
much like that of the Commune, must be our method
to-day.   That does not mean to say that this same
method and this same reserve must be employed in
present day Germany, as was the case in the Commune
of 1871 in Paris.   Since then, half a century of the
most powerful capitalistic development has elapsed.
The enormous progress that was made is shown by
the fact that, at that time, it was Paris alone which
rose in an insurrection that was not purely proletarian,
without any support from the country; and that it had
to succumb to the superiority of agrarianism, which
was intimately bound up with bureaucracy and higher
finance.   In the year 1918 the German Revolution
broke out throughout the entire Empire, and it was
everywhere led by the proletariat.   German agriculture
constitutes hardly more than a quarter of the population (1907—29 per cent.), and industry has made
enormous progress and has advanced to the formation
of Trade Unions comprising whole branches of
industry.

The Parisian proletariat in 1871 had only just emerged from the Bonaparte regime, which had hitherto prevented it from acquiring any means of education or of organisation. The German proletariat entered on this Revolution with the political and corporate experience of half a century, with political and economic organisation, which embraced millions of people. And finally, the Socialists of Paris in 1871 were on the point of giving up an economic theory that had proved to be unsatisfactory. But they had not gone so far as to evolve another and superior theory. German Socialism has at its command the historical and economic insight and the clear methods of a theory, which has been recognised by the Socialists of all countries as the highest and best, and which even the bourgeois classes accept, thanks to its enormous superiority over any other conception of economics now prevailing. In these circumstances Socialism can proceed much more rapidly, more energetically and with quicker results than was ever possible in 1871.

CENTRALISATION AND FEDERALISM.

We have already spoken of an economic method of the Commune. But we have shown that such a method in the real sense of the word was not to be found. It is impossible to speak of a well-considered and well-planned method in the Commune. For this reason alone, that in the Commune so many opposing forces were endeavouring to work together. The method of procedure in the Commune was the result of opposition, and not of a definite theory. The Socialists themselves in the Commune were not very clear and definite, and they represented only the minority. Nevertheless their spirit and conception of things ruled the economic ideas of Paris at the time. Whereas, however, the majority attached little

importance to economics, and felt themselves even
more insecure than did the minority, with politics in
the Commune it was different. The opposition that
arose in the Commune over politics was far greater.
This opposition seriously influenced and almost destroyed the capacity of the Commune for work, but the
general tendencies arising therefrom gradually found a
middle course, which Marx also accepted, as he did
the methods of procedure in regard to economics. We
know already that the majority of the Commune consisted of Jacobins and Blanquistes. When they
entered the Commune of Paris they hoped to influence
the whole life of France similar to the manner of
1793. They were Radical Republicans and free-
thinkers; they wished to destroy the whole apparatus
of monarchy, of the clerical system as well as the
bureaucracy, and the standing army; and yet they
could have arrived at the supreme command of Paris
only by means of a State organisation, which would
have made one of the central positions in Paris a
strong means of force. They forgot that the Paris
Commune of 1793, by means of the centralised power
which was thereby developed, actually prepared the
way for Bonaparte and the Empire. They hoped to
get salvation by means of dictatorial power, without
realising that a dictatorship, which is not supported
by sternly disciplined armies and organised administration, is the mere shadow of a dictatorship. In
strong opposition to the centralising Jacobins were the
Proudhonistes, who were extremely critical of the traditions of 1793, which they in fact abhorred. They
realised the illusions which led to the Reign of Terror,
and which befooled the proletariat and made it bloodthirsty and brutal, without in the least aiding it
towards freedom. But they were not less critical
towards democracy. Universal suffrage in 1848 had
helped to create the reactionary National Assembly,
and had become the main support of the Empire.

Indeed, in the economic conditions of France at that time the State policy, whether of the dictatorship or of the democracy, could offer no hope for the immediate emancipation of the proletariat. A means towards this end was sought by the Socialists. The idea of development in general, as well as of the significance which democracy might have for the development of political insight and the organising capacity of the proletariat, and ultimately for its emancipation—to this idea they were completely strange. For the immediate emancipation of the proletariat at that time neither the dictatorship nor the democracy was very hopeful. This the Proudhonistes understood very well; but the consequences they drew from this were not good. Entirely without a policy such as they wished, they found it was impossible for them to proceed. At this time the communal policy in certain industrial municipalities offered the proletariat quite other prospects than those offered by the State policy in a country which was preponderantly agrarian. Democracy in the districts was of great importance; in the State it was of small account. The bitter critics of the State Parliaments, of these " talking shops," as they called them, had nothing to say against the communal talking shops and Parliaments. The sovereignty of the municipality became the ideal of the Proudhonistes. Their idea is shown already in the status of industry as they regarded it. Moreover, they did not intend to do away with exchange; for even at that time there were business concerns, whose economic importance extended far beyond the single community. In order to control such concerns, it was necessary for the different municipalities to combine. In this way the Proudhonistes hoped to emancipate the industrial proletariat and agrarian France. But they forgot one small thing, namely, that the idea of dissolving the State into sovereign municipalities was also a State idea, to carry out which the overthrow of the existing

State was necessary, which was exactly what the proletariat wished to avoid. The idea of the Commune, in the Proudhonist sense, was therefore the direct contrary to the idea such as the Jacobins held. For the Jacobin, the Commune of Paris was a means to obtain State power for the control of the whole of France. For the Proudhonist, the sovereignty of each Commune was a means to putting an end to State power as such.

Arthur Arnould characterises very well this contrast of the revolutionary Jacobins and the " Socialist Federalists " in his book, " Histoire Populaire et Parliamentaire de la Commune de Paris.'' The same words were often understood by the different members of the Assembly in two quite different ways. " For one group, the Commune of Paris represented the first application of anti-government principle, the war against the old conception of the centralised despotic single State. The Commune represented for them the triumph of the principle of autonomy, of the free federation of groups, and of the most direct form of government ' of the people by the people '; but in their eyes the Commune formed the first stage of a great revolution, social as well as political, which had nothing to do with the old methods of procedure. It was the very negation of the idea of a dictatorship. It was the seizure of power by the people themselves, and therefore the destruction of every power that stood outside the people or over them. The people, who so felt and thought and willed, represented that group which afterwards was called the Socialist Group, or the Minority. For the others, on the other hand, the Commune of Paris was the continuation of the old Commune of 1793. In their eyes it represented dictatorship in the name of the people, an enormous concentration of power in the hands of a few, and the destruction of the old system through the setting up of new men at the head of the system, whom, for the moment, they provided with arms to fight a war in the service of the people against the enemy of the people.

"Among the men of this authoritative group, the idea of the centralised individual State had by no means disappeared. If they accepted the principle of municipal autonomy and the free federation of groups, and even proclaimed this on their banners, they did so solely because the will of Paris forced them. They remained slaves to old habits and thoughts. As soon as they came into power, they continued in their old habits and allowed themselves, certainly with the best of intentions, to employ old methods to new ideas. They did not realise that in such cases the former always gains the victory in the struggle, and that those who try to establish freedom by means of the dictatorship, or of mere arbitrariness, generally destroy that which they would save. This group, which consisted of many various elements, formed the majority, and they were called ' The Revolutionary Jacobins.' "

Debreuilh has quoted these comments with the remark that they referred only to the two extreme tendencies. That is true. It is equally true that in all such tendencies many new shades of opinion are to be found. Still, if we wish to have a clear idea of them we must regard the most pronounced characteristic as if it were the classical characteristic. The opposition that existed was enormous. It might never have been overcome had the Commune been victorious. But it was not victorious, and that forced the contending parties to strike out some fresh line. From April 3rd onwards the Commune found itself on the defensive, and had to surrender all idea of conquering France and ruling it. In this way all the Jacobin hopes fell to the ground. Far from hoping to rule through the Commune, they had to be content if they succeeded merely in preventing the new-found liberties of Paris from being crushed by reactionary France.

But in those circumstances there was just as little
hope that the Proudhonist dreams would be fulfilled,
that the French State would crumble to pieces, and
that complete sovereignty would be bestowed on the
separate municipalities.   The Centralising Jacobins,
like the Federalist Proudhonistes, were obliged by the
force of circumstances to work for the same object,
which would be realisable under favourable circumstances, which became of paramount importance for
the whole of France, and was even demanded by many
of its citizens and politicians.   This object was, namely,
the self-control of the municipalities, their independence within limits drawn by the State democracy,
and the limitation of the power of State bureaucracy,
as well as the setting up of a militia in place of the
standing army.   The Internationalists recognised this
democratic State all the more readily, because, as we
have seen, they were drawn into a fight against the
Empire in those latter years, and therefore were
involved in a State policy and had begun to carry out
strict Proudhonism mingled with Marxist ideas.
    The final result was a policy, which Marx himself
would have recognised and sanctioned if he had been
in Paris; but he would not have been able to join either
the one or the other party.   He would have been quite
isolated.   Nevertheless, force of circumstances and the
wisdom of the best heads of the Commune, who really
took into consideration the actual '' circumstances ''
and were not driven by '' mere will,'' resulted in the
striking out of a line of policy, which showed much
resemblance to that of Marx himself.   To this
policy, still more than to its economic measures,
Mendelssohn's remark well applies (in his appendix
to Lissagaray, page 525): '' The creators of the
Commune seem not to know what they have created.''
    The political order of things newly created by the
Commune, amidst the bitterest internal struggles,
proceeded on lines between the two extremes.   The

great misfortune from which the Commune suffered
was its lack of organisation. It was the natural outcome of the lack of organisation, routine and ability in
the Parisian proletariat at the time, which had really
only just broken away from the Empire. The
Commune, from the very beginning, stood in a state of
war with Versailles. Nowhere are organisation and
discipline more necessary than in war. They were
completely failing in the Commune. The battalions
of the Commune were commanded by officers whom
those battalions themselves had elected. In this way
the officers were independent of the supreme command,
but were dependent on those who had chosen them.
On these lines it is impossible to organise a real fighting army, for such an army is only possible where
internal disorganisation is forbidden.

This is what the Bolsheviks in Russia have seen, for
they very soon put an end to the powers of the Soldiers'
Councils and of the election of officers through the men,
when they found themselves involved in a really serious
war. Whether or not the different battalions of the
National Guard obeyed the orders of the supreme command depended entirely upon their mood. Small
wonder, therefore, that the number of actual fighters
in the Commune was very small. Pay was made to
162,000 men and 6,500 officers, but the number of
those who went into the fire and fought varied after
those fatal days of April 3rd from 20,000 to 30,000.
These brave fellows had to sustain the whole fearful
burden of battle against a well-disciplined and well-
equipped superior force, which in the second half of
the month of May numbered at least 120,000 men.
Disorganisation from below was still more increased by
disorganisation from above. Alongside of the Commune, the Central Committee of the National Guard
continued to exist. It had formally handed over all
its power to the Commune. Nevertheless, it continued
to intervene in all orders given to the National Guard.

Marx, in a letter to Kugelmann, on the Commune of April 12th, 1871, regards it as a mistake that the Central Committee so early abandoned its power in order to make room for the Commune ('' Neue Zeit,'' XX., page 709). He does not give the ground for this statement, and we therefore cannot tell why this seemed to him to be a mistake—apparently on account of the reaction of the conduct of the war. He regards this mistake as the second one made by the Parisians. The first mistake, according to him, consisted in their not having marched against Versailles immediately after March 18th. These two mistakes may have been the cause of defeat. In the meantime, unfortunately, all these fundamental mistakes, which made the military situation of the Commune from the very start so hopeless, were made already, before the Commune ever assembled. Nothing can show that the conduct of the war, under the command of the Central Committee, would have met with any more success than it had under the Command of the Commune. On the contrary, that Committee showed itself to be more vacillating even than the Commune. The conduct of war is not the proletariat's strongest point.

The worst that happened, however, was the existence of two simultaneous independent supreme powers, to which was added yet a third, which interfered with the carrying on of the war, namely, the '''Committee of Artillery.'' The Committee of Artillery, which was formed on March 18th, made trouble with the Ministry of War over the cannons. The Ministry of War was in possession of the cannons of Marsfeld, whereas the Artillery Committee had those of Montmartre. (Lissagaray, '' History of the Commune,'' page 205.)

Everywhere an attempt was made to minimise the general organisation, by strengthening the power of the Government. In place of the Executive Commissions, of which we have already spoken, there was formed,

on April 20th, an Executive Council consisting of nine
men, each of whom was a delegate from each of the
nine Commissions. But the evil was too deep-rooted
to be removed by such a measure.   The Jacobins,
mindful of the traditions of 1793, demanded a Committee of Public Safety with dictator's powers, which
would reduce the Commune to nothing.   The continuous adventures of the Versailles troops caused the
member of the Commune, Miot, "who had one of the
finest beards of 1848" (Lissagaray, page 273) to
demand on April 28th the formation of a Committee of
Public Safety, in other words, of a new Commission,
which should be over all other Commissions.   As to
the necessity for a powerful executive everybody was
in agreement, although the question of a name for
that executive caused heated debate.   The Revolutionary Jacobins thought that if this Commission was
called the Committee of Public Safety, it would
bestow on that Committee the victorious power of the
French Republic of 1793, with its Committee of Public
Safety.   But this very tradition, which brought into
remembrance the Regiment of Terror, repelled the
Proudhonistes. With 34 votes against 20 it was decided
on May 1st to form this Committee.   In the election,
which led to its formation the greater part of the
minority, 23, abstained, giving the following explana-
tion :

"We have not set up any candidate. We did not
want anybody who appeared to us to be as injurious
as he would be useless; for we see in this Committee
of Public Safety the denial of the principles of Social
reform, out of which the Communal Revolution of
March 18th arose."

This Committee of Public Safety, which was to lead
to increased energy on the part of the Commune, at
the same time prepared the way for its disorganisation.
In fact, it split the Commune. For this reason alone
the Committee lost all moral power, and further, those

who alone performed any serious work in the Commune, namely the Nationalists, held aloof from it.
Its members were all, with the exception of one,
"bawlers," as Lissagaray expressed it. On May 9th
this futile Committee was disposed of, in order that a
new one might be elected. This time the Minority took
part in the election, after it had seen that behind the
much-feared name there was lurking nothing less than
an actual dictatorship. But meanwhile the opposition
between the Majority and the Minority had become
so acute, that the Majority made the extraordinary
mistake of not electing one member of the Minority
to the Committee. The second Committee of Public
Safety proved to be as incapable as the first. It even
went further than the first, by actively rising against
the Minority, and removing a certain number of the
Minority from office, thus robbing the Commune of
some of its best men. This led to an open breach. On
May 16th the Minority published in the papers a
declaration, in which they protested against the abdica-
tion of the Commune in favour of an irresponsible
dictatorship, and announced that, from that time onwards, they would no longer take part in the work of the
Commune, and would confine their activities solely to
the districts and to the National Guard. In this way,
they said, in conclusion, they hoped to save the Commune from internal strife, which they wished to avoid,
because the Majority and the Minority were both working towards the same purpose. In spite of this conciliatory conclusion, it seemed that this declaration
implied a complete rupture.

Nevertheless, although the Minority, for administrative work as well as for the solution of economic
problems, was a good deal more capable than the
Majority, in its politics it was not very decisive or
logical. Against the dictatorship of the first Committee
of Public Safety it had protested by abstaining from
voting on May 1st. But on May 9th it had already

recognised the dictatorship by proposing candidates for the Second Committee. On the 15th, again, they decided to make public protest against this same dictatorship, by stopping all collaboration in the Commune. On the 16th, the day of the publication of their protest, they yielded to the pressure of their friends, namely, of the Federal Council of the International, who urged them not to destroy the unity of the Commune in face of the insistent enemy; and so on the 17th fifteen of the twenty-two subscribers to the manifesto were again in their places in the Committee. But the majority was not by this means appeased, in spite of the attempt at reconciliation made by some of the more reasonable of their members, including Vaillant. A resolution, conciliatory in character, was refused, and a proposal of Miot's was accepted, which ran as follows :

" The Commune will forget the attitude of every member of the Minority, who withdraws his signature from the declaration. It blames this declaration."
Debreuilh remarks in connection with this, (page 440) :
" Thus Jacobins and Federalists stood together as enemy brothers at the last battle before their death."

On May 21st the Versailles troops entered Paris. On the 22nd the last sitting of the Commune took place.

The policy of the Commune offers us a remarkable spectacle. Of the two tendencies which are represented in the Commune each was guided by a programme, which, had it been applied, could never have been carried out, and which only led its disciples to actions that were purposeless. But in spite of all this, the action and reaction of these two programmes on one another, as the result of the force of circumstances, produced a political programme, which was not only capable of being carried out, but which corresponded to the needs of France at the time, and which even to-day has latent within it the most fruitful possibilities. This programme consisted of a demand for self-administration of the municipalities, as well as for the dissolution of the standing army. These two fundamental demands of the Commune are to-day no less important for the welfare of France than they were at the time of the Second Paris Commune.

Terrorist Ideas of the Commune.

We cannot speak of the Committee of Public Safety without thinking of the Regiment of Terror, which represented the very soul of that body in 1793.   It was only natural that the opposition arising over the dictatorship of the Committee of Public Safety should find its continuation in the question of terrorism. The Jacobins were, from the very start, as much in favour of recognising terrorism as a fighting means as the Internationalists were of repudiating it.   Even in the very first meeting of the Commune its opposition was noticeable.   A member proposed the abolition of the death penalty.   '' He wants to save the head of Venoy '' (the General of Versailles), was the retort they levelled at him.

Before the federation of the International, Frankel formulated on April 29th the policy of the International, saying: '' We wish to establish the rights of the workers, and that is only possible by persuasion and moral force.''

On the other side were people like the dramatic critic Pyat, the accountant Ferré, and the student Raoul Rigault, who in their bloodthirsty demands were insatiable.   In principle all Jacobins had to support Terrorist measures, but in actual practice there was little of these measures to be seen.   Few could escape the humanitarian spirit which inspired the whole of democracy, bourgeois as well as proletarian.   Moreover, the conditions which obtained at the time of the

Second Paris Commune were not those that produced
Terrorism at the time of the First Commune.

The Second Commune did not set about the
impossible task of erecting a communal system on
bourgeois lines which should serve the interests of the
proletariat, and, further, it confined the application
of its power to Paris, of which city the majority were
certainly on its side. Thus it was not necessary for
them to intimidate their opponents by resorting to
forceful measures. The enemy who was really dangerous to the Commune stood outside the confines of
their communal life, and was not to be affected by
recourse to Terrorism. Thus the motive for putting
Terrorist tradition into practice was lacking. What
Raoul Rigault and Ferré in the Committee of Public
Safety accomplished by their suppression of the Press
and by their arrests was much more a mere bad
imitation of the Empire than of the Reign of Terror,
which proceeded on entirely different lines. The
Blanquiste student, Rigault, gained his laurels under
the Empire in a continuous fight with the police,
whose tricks he knew perfectly well.

Even before March 9, that is, before the insurrection,
Lauser said of him : " Those who know him have told
me the most astonishing things about his mad ways,
and the cunning with which he spied out the police
to frustrate all their persecutions, and indeed himself
to play the part of the Prefect of Police of Paris."
(" Under the Paris Commune—a Diary," Leipsig,
1878, page 18.)

On March 18 he had received official orders to act as
the Prefect of Police of Paris. His first act was to
take up a position at the Prefecture of Police on the
night of March 18. His police system very soon met
with lively opposition from all parties, but especially
from the Internationalists. This system had little to
do with the principles of 1793, although at the time
he was working on a History of the Commune of 1793.

On the other hand, we must not attribute the execution of Generals Thomas and Clement to the Commune. As we have already shown, these executions took place before the Commune existed and in spite of the opposition of the Central Committee.

There was only one measure adopted by the Commune which can be described as Terrorist, and that was the arresting of hostages, undertaken to intimidate the enemy by oppressing the defenceless. That the taking of hostages is a hopeless method of procedure, which seldom prevents cruelties from taking place, and more often increases the barbarity of the fight which caused it, has often enough been proved in experience.

But it was difficult for the Commune to do anything else, unless it wished to suffer patiently and without protest that the men at Versailles should shoot the prisoners they had taken. In numerous cases this actually took place after April 3rd.

'' As the result of the indignation, which arose on account of the execution of the prisoners Puteaux and Chatillon, as well as of Duval, who was one of the officers of the National Guard taken prisoner by the Versailles troops during the attack on April 3, several members of the Commune insisted that one should forthwith shoot a number of the reactionaries, who, for the most part, were taken from the clergy of Paris. Other Jacobins, and particularly Delescluse, indignant at these excesses, proposed the decree concerning hostages. It was decided to oppose the Versailles elements on the bloody way into which they had blindly stumbled. By means of an implicit understanding, however, it was agreed that this decree should not be carried out.'' (Fiaux, '' Civil War of 1871,'' page 246.)

This decree, therefore, arose not out of an attempt to *destroy* human life, but to *save* it. On the one hand, to force the Versailles commanders to stop all further executions, and on the other, to make the Prussians renounce the idea of immediate reprisals.

" Ever noble and righteous even in its anger," so ran the proclamation of the Commune of April 5th, " the people view with horror the shedding of blood as well as civil war. But it is its duty to defend itself from barbaric attacks of its enemies; it must therefore act on the principle of an eye for an eye and a tooth for a tooth." (*Journal Officiel*, April 6th, page 169.)

In reality the Commune showed itself to be very noble and righteous, but it did not act in accordance with the principle of an eye for an eye and a tooth for a tooth!

The decree issued by the Commune concerning hostages determined that any persons accused of being in agreement with Versailles should be immediately denounced and arrested. A court of justice was to be set up within the space of twenty-four hours to hear the accused, and within forty-eight hours pass judgment on him. No accused person was to be shot, but kept as hostage. Likewise all prisoners of war were to be brought before this same tribunal, which would thereupon decide whether they were to be set free or detained as hostages. Finally, it was decided that every execution practised on a fighter or follower of the Commune, who had been caught by the Versailles command, should be followed by the execution of three times the number of hostages. This last and most terrible decision of the decree really remained a dead letter. It was never put into practice by the Commune, although those in command at Versailles, after short interruptions, continued to shoot the prisoners they had caught, and seemed quite unconcerned by the fact that, by their action, they had jeopardised the lives of their friends, who had been kept as hostages in Paris. Thiers did his best to incite the Commune to slaughter. He knew perfectly well that every hostage shot rendered a service, not to the

Commune, but to himself; because it roused public
opinion at large, which was still governed by bourgeois
thought and feeling, and coolly accepted the shooting of numberless prisoners at Versailles, whereas
it waxed violently indignant over the mere arresting of
hostages in Paris. This miserable attitude was shown
by Thiers in the affair of the exchange of hostages.

After the decree of April 5th, there were taken
as hostages in Paris a number of the clergy, a banker,
Jecker, the originator of the Mexican Expedition, as
well as the President of the Cour de Cassation, Bonjean.
But the Commune proposed an exchange. They
wished to set at liberty the arrested clergy, among
them the Archbishop Darboy, the Pastor Deguerry,
and the Vicar-General Lagarde, as well as President
Bonjean, provided the Versailles Government would
deliver up Blanqui, who was then under arrest. They
were good-natured enough to allow the Vicar-General
Lagarde to proceed to Versailles on April 12th with a letter of Darboy's to Thiers, after he had sworn to return if
the deliberations should come to grief. But before that,
on April 8th, Darboy had already addressed a letter to
Thiers, and implored him to shoot no more prisoners.
Thiers remained silent. On April 13th a Paris news-
paper, *L'Affranchi*, published this letter. Whereupon
Thiers replied; but with a lie, since he characterised
all news about executions as being mere libel. The
answer to the second letter, which Lagarde had handed
in, was not received until the end of April. But the
Vicar-General, in spite of his oath, was cautious
enough not to return to brave the vengeance of the
lion. In this answer Blanqui's release was refused,
but the Archbishop was comforted with the assurance
that the lives of hostages were not in danger. Further
attempts on the part of the Papal Nuncio and of the
American Ambassador, Washburn, to intervene in
favour of an exchange remained equally without
success. Therefore Thiers was responsible for the fact

that the above-named, with the exception of Lagarde, were still to be found as hostages in the prisons of Mazas, when the Commune broke up and lost the power to protect them.   He was quite right in his assertion which, by the way, entirely disproved his libellous statement about the brutality of the Commune, that the lives of the hostages in the Commune were not in danger.   But it was he himself who laboured to overthrow the protecting bodyguard of the hostages, namely the regiment of the Commune, indeed, under circumstances which placed the lives of these hostages in the gravest danger.   Through some treacherous act, the Versailles troops forced their way into Paris on a Sunday, May 21st, quite by surprise, at the very time when a popular concert was in full swing in the Garden of the Tuileries, and at the conclusion of which concert an officer of the General Staff invited the audience to come again the following Sunday, adding:

" Thiers promised to march into Paris yesterday. He did not come, nor will he ever come."   At that very moment the Versailles troops entered Paris.   The inhabitants were so panic stricken, and the troops of the Commune so exhausted, that the Versailles army would probably have succeeded, by means of a rapid and determined advance, in occupying the whole of Paris without any serious opposition.   But they entered very slowly, and this gave the defenders of the Commune time to gather together for a furious street fight, which lasted the whole of the week, the famous " terrible May week."   This succeeded all the more in bringing passions to fever heat, since the Versailles commanders gave no pardon, and not only shot down all those who were arrested with weapons in their hands, but even all the suspects.   Many historians of the Commune point out that this slow advance of the Versailles troops had the result of increasing the opposition, and likewise the number of those who fell, thus enhancing the immensity of the defeat.

" Paris could have been taken in twenty-four hours if the army had proceeded along the quays of the left bank. It would have met with opposition only from the Ministry of Marine at Montmartre and at Ménilmontant. By means of its slow advance into Paris it gave time for the opposition to organise. They made eight and ten times as many prisoners as there were fighters, and they shot more men than actually stood behind the barricades, whereas the army lost only 600 dead and 7,000 wounded." (G. Bourgin, " L'Histoire de la Commune," page 108.)

The number of dead on the side of the Commune exceeded 20,000, put by some at 30,000. The Chief of Military Justice, General Appert, counted 17,000 dead. The number of victims who did not come to the knowledge of the authorities cannot be fixed, but amounted to at least 3,000.

It is not to be wondered at that, in this fearful storm, the thirst for vengeance in many cases gained the upper hand. It became the more furious the more power it lost and the less able it was to avoid defeat. It was only after the Commune had ceased to exist that the execution of hostages began. On May 21st the Versailles troops entered Paris; on the 22nd street fighting began; on the 24th the last shot was fired. In this respect, although the executions were more the result of desperate rage and blind revenge than of premeditated action, the opposition between Jacobins and the Internationalists became obvious. The beginning of the executions was made by the fanatic Blanquist, Raoul Rigault. He ordered a number of gendarmes, who were arrested on March 18, along with an editor, by name Chaudey, caught in the middle of April, to be executed on the night of May 23. Chaudey had caused the crowd to be fired upon on January 22, during which affray Sapia, a friend of

Rigault, was killed by his side. On the 24th Rigault himself was arrested and shot. At the same time the old Blanquist, Genton, demanded the execution of six hostages, among them the Archbishop Darboy, President Bonjean, and Pastor Dugeurry, already known to us. The Blanquist, Ferré, gave him the authority.

" The firing party of the execution was composed almost exclusively of young people, practically children. In most cases those taking part in these crimes were hardly more than adolescent young men, excited through the vice rampant in the towns, and whose passions, which had grown faster than their beards, left no place open for the feeling of responsibility." (Fiaux, " Civil War," page 528.)

Unfortunately we cannot make the same observation to-day in Germany in the case of those who would justify by practice the right of war.

On the 26th it was again the Blanquist, Ferré, who arranged that forty-eight hostages, mostly priests, secret police, and gendarmes, who had fired on the crowd on March 18th, should be handed over to Colonel Gois, likewise a Blanquist. He took them along with him, followed by an armed crowd who were in utter disorder, since they could hope for no pardon, and since they were themselves doomed to death. In desperate rage they fell upon the hostages and killed them one after the other. In vain the Internationalists, Varlin and Serailler, tried to rescue them. They themselves were very nearly lynched by the furious crowd, who accused them of belonging to the Versailles Party. On May 28th this same Varlin, who had risked his life to save the hostages, was arrested by the Versailles command as a result of the denunciation of a priest, who had recognised him in the street, and he was forthwith shot.

Of the countless victims who succumbed to the murderous lusts of the victors, both during the fight and after it, those bourgeois elements that waxed indignant over the terrorism of the Commune had nothing to say. On the contrary, they had not words enough to express their furious condemnation, when they came to speak of the five dozen hostages who, after the downfall of the Commune, fell victims to the vengeance and irresponsibility of some of the Versailles Party.

It is this very account of the affair with the hostages that proves most clearly how far removed the Commune was from any form of terrorism. In the whole of history there is no mention of a civil war, hardly of a national war, in which one side, in spite of the murderous inhumanity of the other side, upheld in practice the principles of humanity with such noble determination, and in such contrast to the blood-thirsty phrases of a few of the "Radicalinskis," such as appeared in the French Civil War of 1871. This is the reason why the Second Paris Commune ended quite differently from the First, which had formed such a fearful Regiment of Terror.

The Regiment of Terror of the First Commune fell to pieces, without the workers of Paris offering any opposition. Indeed, its fall was felt as a relief by some, and by many even greeted with satisfaction. When, on the Ninth Thermidor, 1794, the forces of the two opposing parties came into contact, the followers of Robespierre turned tail before a single shot was fired, and fled. On the other hand, the Parisians clung to the Second Paris Commune with fanatical tenacity to the very end. The fiercest street fighting was necessary for a whole week, before it could be overcome. The number of victims, of dead, wounded, prisoners and escaped, which resulted from the death struggle of the Commune, reached the number of 100,000. (In July, 1871, the number was put at 90,000—Bourgin, "La Commune," page 183.)

The Second Commune was torn asunder by violent opposition. We have seen this in the enmity of the two parties engaged in the last struggle. But never did one of these parties ever oppress the other by terrorist means. The Maximalists ('' Bolshevik '' means Maximalist in English) and the Minimalists (Russian '' Mensheviks '') fought together, in spite of all, to the bitter end; and so all factions of Socialism in the Commune foresaw the necessity of common representation of the whole of the fighting proletariat. In recognising this they combined the views of Marx and Bakunin, Lassalle and Eisenach. The first government of the proletariat has engraved itself deep in the hearts of those who craved for the emancipation of humanity. The powerful effect of this '' dictatorship of the proletariat '' on the fight for emancipation in all countries was due, not a little, to the fact that it was inspired throughout with a spirit of humanity, which animated the working classes of the nineteenth century.

CHAPTER VII.

THE EFFECT OF CIVILISATION ON HUMAN CUSTOMS.

BRUTALITY AND HUMANITY.

WE have seen that the massacres of the great French Revolution were not repeated in succeeding revolutions; that from 1830 to 1871 the revolutionary fighters, even when they were under the influence of the traditions established by the Regiment of Terror, nevertheless in practice strove to be as humane as possible—in contrast to their enemies who, both before and after, developed the worst form of brutality in June, 1848, as much as in May, 1871.

During the whole of the nineteenth century we can observe a progressive humanising taking place among the working classes. Now, at the beginning of the twentieth century, the Revolution in Russia and Germany has come, and has given rein to massacres, which remind us of the French Revolution of the eighteenth century. How can we explain this reversal? According to general ideas, humanity is a product of culture. We assume that man is by nature an evil unsociable creature, with the instincts of beasts of prey, ever ready to attack his neighbour, to oppress him, to torture and kill him. We believe further, that it is only after long progress in education and training, in other words, in civilisation, that man acquires social sentiment, a sense of mutual assistance and of kindness, as well as of abhorrence of cruelty and murder.

This idea is expressed in the language we employ, which uses the word "humanity" to describe those qualities that we have just mentioned, and dis-

tinguishes them from those other features, which are
stigmatised as bestial ("bestia," the beast) and brutal
("brutus," the brute.)   A great number of our ethno-
logists share this point of view, which is also that
adopted by Lombroso and his school, who see in violent
crime what they call atavism, a drop back into the
sensient life of the animal precursors of man.   Moreover, even bloodthirsty beasts of prey do not, as a rule,
kill their own kind ; and nothing justifies us in assuming
that man is really by nature a beast of prey, with
violent bloodthirsty instincts.   We know nothing about
the animal precursors of the human species, but we
must assume that, among the animals of the present
day, the human ape approaches them most nearly.
Like these, the ancestor of man apparently lived on
vegetable nourishment, which he occasionally supple-
mented   with   small   animals,   caterpillars,   worms,
reptiles, even small birds; but he never killed a large
mammal in order to devour it.   No ape does the like.

In the first place, the ape never carries on any
murderous war against its own kind.   From the very
start, he has not the necessary organs for such.   Single
creatures may indulge in fights over their booty, or over
a wife, and receive scratches. but these scrimmages do
not end fatally.

All this is changed in the case of man, as soon as his
technical knowledge provides him with materials in
addition to his natural organs, with tools and weapons
of shell and sword.   In this way he acquires the faculties of a beast of prey, and their development in him
gives   him   all   the   functions   and   instincts   of   a
beast of prey.   Now he can kill larger animals and
rend them.   Vegetable nourishment thus loses its
importance for him.   The hunt and the shedding of
blood become for him daily occupations.   In this way,
conflicts between two single individuals may lead to
death.   Nevertheless, the murder of whole peoples,
namely war, cannot be explained by the invention of

weapons alone. War presupposes a further cultivated development, namely, the grouping of people into close communities.

Since this point has hitherto been very little considered, and as I myself have hitherto not treated it sufficiently, a few remarks may here be made, although they lead us somewhat away from our subject. Without doubt man takes his origin from the social animals, but he distinguishes himself from them by the fact that he forms close communities. The social animals, as a rule, live in flocks and herds, which have very little internal cohesion. According to the conditions of life, to the supply of food, to the number of enemies, etc., these same individual creatures sometimes form themselves into immense herds. Another time they are split up into many small groups, and even into mere couples, until some more favourable opportunity brings them together again in large masses. Without any difficulty one individual can pass from one group to another. With man it is utterly different. It would lead us too far here to discuss to what this change is due, but the following short remarks may be made.

The animals' means of communication between one another are dependent on the natural noises, which they instinctively make, as also on the method of speech contained in gesture and mimicry, which, however, they do not have to learn from each other, but which are innate in them. Hence every member of the community can equally well express itself in this manner, and be understood by all.

What distinguishes human beings from animals, apart from the use of tools, is articulated speech. Besides these tools, which are not given him at birth, but which he himself fashions, and the construction of which he must learn from his neighbours, there is a further means of understanding, which likewise is not born with him, but which his fellow-beings have developed as a result of their environment, and which he himself must learn from them. This means of communication is not given to the whole community from the start, but is differently formed in different places. Through this method of speech, social unity becomes stronger and more intimate, since, through it, understanding and community of labour are rendered easier and more varied. Through these differences the several tribes and groups of mankind are, from the very start, kept apart one from the other. Therefore each will be forced to remain with that particular tribe or group whose speech he has learnt. He cannot communicate with others. He feels strange and uncomfortable when he is among them. In addition to this another factor arises. Speech permits single individuals to establish their relations with one another. It also permits memories of the past to be recorded. In other words, it forms a conservative element. The fully developed animal easily forgets its parents and the members of its family, which it is unable to distinguish from other creatures of its kind. But the human being, his whole life long, can preserve these relations. He can even recognise and remember the parents of his own parents and the children of his own children, as well as the children of his brothers and sisters, and so on.

It is generally assumed that the family is something ordained by nature, and that the " voice of blood " is proof of this fact. In reality it is the " voice of speech " that is created. Without some indication of relationship no family can exist as a permanent institution. " The voice of blood " ceases in the case of animals, so soon as the young creatures are fledged and have become independent. This makes it all the more ridiculous, when people of to-day attempt to explain not only *family*, but even *national* ties as being the result of the " voice of blood "; as, for instance, when the impulse of the German Austrians towards union with the Germans of the Empire is given as an example of the secret law of this "voice." Actually in German Austria there are living more men of non-German origin, especially Czechs, than men directly connected with the German Empire.

The intimate nature of a family was further enhanced by the formation of households and by the accumulation of private property in the shape of tools and weapons, utensils of all kinds, which survive the possessor. For, after his death, all such private property went to those members of the family who lived in closest communication with him, and was therefore a good reason for maintaining the permanency of this communication to his death. The intimacy of the stock was further preserved through possessions of another kind, that is, through the possession of the land, which was the common property of the stock. Even animals prefer to live in those parts in which they have been brought up, and where they are, so to speak, at home; in which every source of food is known to them, every corner, and every dangerous spot. Nevertheless, the limits of such parts are not very closely drawn, and an individual member of the stock, which cannot find sufficient food in the locality, or because of danger in some way, can without difficulty extend the range of his sphere, until he comes into a different region that pleases him better. But there, sooner or later, he attaches himself to another tribe.

This is different in the more intimate societies of human beings. Whoever comes into another province finds himself among a group of men and women he cannot understand. Primitive man does not adapt himself to new conditions by passing into new regions thinly populated, and there settling. This adaptation is to be found only in a higher state of culture, and even there in an imperfect state. On the contrary, the herd or stock keeps together, and seeks to extend its sphere at the cost of its neighbours. Thus

we have the beginnings of war, and of race
murder, as soon as the technique of armies
has become sufficiently highly developed. Thus
we see what we call "brutality" is not due to the
animal precursors of man, but is rather a product of
his development. Ethical instincts themselves, the
feeling for solidarity, of sympathy for others, of
rendering assistance, in the course of man's development change their character. In the case of the social
animals, these instincts are shared in common by all
the individual members of like species.

In the case of man, however, their sphere of
influence is confined to the members of the immediate
circle. Whoever is outside this circle is, for such a
man, an object of indifference. He has no sympathy
for him and is often directly hostile. As inter-communi-
cation develops, the sphere of society, a member of
which our "individual man" feels himself to be, is enlarged also. To-day we are, as it were, reverting to the
origins of human development; and the sphere of our
social and ethical feelings is again beginning to extend
itself to all individuals of like species, in other words,
to the whole human race. But, generally speaking,
this is more an ideal towards which we are very slowly
striving. At the same time, economic development,
through the division of labour and increasing variety
of social communications, has led to the constitution
of single, circumscribed societies within the State,
which again, in its turn, is broken up into groups of
varying kinds. These also become more or less
separate communities, such as the nobility, families,
ecclesiastical organisations, sects, guilds, etc. Each of
these communities develops its own ethical ideals,
which have effect only on the members of each particular community. And even these different communities can fall into disagreement with one another.
They are capable of developing great solidarity and
sympathy for members of their own narrow group, at

the same time showing a complete lack of charity towards other groups.   Each individual may belong to several different social communities, with different and often opposing interests and ethical principles. The sharper the contradiction within the society, the greater will be the opposition between individual men. The ladies of the feudal barons of the South States were most charming and adorable to others of their cwn kind, full of generosity and sympathy; but their slaves they tortured unmercifully.   The same man can show the most delicate feeling for the members of his family, and yet in his business relations be the most callous extortioner and pitiless taskmaster.

Culture does not necessarily, at the same time, help towards the humanising of conduct.   On the other hand, it would be absurd to assume the contrary, and to regard the primitive state of nature as an idyllic condition of the Golden Age, from which we have been gradually falling away.   In this connection we can distinguish two conflicting tendencies in the history of human development, of which either the one or the other becomes paramount according to the conditions at the time.

Two Tendencies.

One tendency we have already discussed.   It consists in the continuous improvement in the weapons for slaughter, as well as in the increasing of the forces of antagonism in man.   It makes for the increase of national opposition, the opposition that arises between over-populated and under-populated regions; further, the opposition between poor people and rich people, between those who monopolise the treasures of nature, and others, who are forced to remain in unfruitful deserts.   It leads, further, to the opposition between the industrially developed and the industrially backward. And finally, among the nations themselves, there arise different forms of expropriation and enslavement of man by man, whence arise hatred and cruelty.

A contrary tendency arises with the beginning of agriculture. In earlier methods of production, hunting and cattle-driving take the upper hand. Both cattle-driving and the hunt necessitate skill in arms, and cause the shedding of blood as a means to the maintenance of life, and as a means of defence against beasts of prey, which threaten the cattle at the dawn of civilisation. Agriculture, on the other hand, does not necessarily employ weapons. The husbandman often sees a friend in the wild beasts, because they attack other beasts of prey, which threaten to devour his crops; and the preserving of wild game, which is of importance to the huntsman, is disliked by the husbandman. Still more than in the case with agriculture is the use of weapons superfluous, as a means of production, in the case of the artisan and the intellectual worker. The time and material required for the fabrication of such weapons, and the learning of their employment is, to such men, in contrast to the huntsman and the cattle breeder, an economic extravagance, which they would reduce as much as possible. Thus the peasant, the artisan, and the intellectual become more and more amicable in nature; especially the last group, for the peasant and the artisan do need muscular strength to carry on their occupation. Such muscular strength stands in high honour with them, and is welcomed, not only in actual work but even in play, and especially in sports that involve competition. The intellectual, on the other hand, needs no other strength. The time the others devote to the development of their muscles he devotes to the acquirement of knowledge, or to the exercise of his brain. Whoever should endeavour to carry on a literary contest with weapons, other than those of the mind, would at once betray his inferiority. This contention is by no means disproved by the fact that, in German student circles, rowdy and bullying manners often come to the fore.   They are the result of the brutal behaviour, characteristic of the religious strife that led up to the Thirty Years' War.

The priestly castes of the ancient world, as well as the spiritual leaders of Christianity, showed, in general, aversion to the shedding of blood and to acts of violence, at any rate so long as they did not belong to the ruling or exploiting classes.   Such also was true of the intellectuals of the eighteenth century.   When, however, the intellectuals themselves became ex-ploiters, they did not always give evidence of the same peaceable tendencies.   Where they are not so inclined, it is the same with them as with the peasants, the artisans, and the proletarians.   Man in such a case is regarded not as a means for the end of others, but as a means for his own ends, or as a means for the ends of the community at large; not, however, as means for the ends of other individuals.   Kant's ethics cor-respond exactly to this standpoint.   Only for Kant ethics do not form a mere moral code for particular classes or times, but rather a permanent moral law, over and beyond the world of appearances, to which the Almighty himself is subject, since even to Him it is forbidden to make use of man as mere means. (For what?)   (Cf. Kant's "Critique of Practical Reason," 2nd edition, section 5, "The existence of God as a postulate of pure practical reason.")

However this attitude may have arisen, there resulted, as a consequence, the greatest respect for human personality, and for the sanctity of human life and human happiness.   But these peace-loving ten-dencies already began to show to disadvantage in the early beginnings of agricultural and communal life, for the peaceable classes of the various nations were the most defenceless.   They were exploited by armed groups, which lauded it over them as a war-like aristocracy, and now, in their turn, with rigorous exclusiveness betook themselves to the hunt, to war and to slaughter, as formerly the huntsman and cattle-breeders had done. So they erected into a principle the methods and instincts of beasts of prey, in their attitude towards their fellow-men who were hostile to them.

Thus brutality and humanity became two characteristics of civilised society. According to changing conditions, either one or the other of these characteristics prevailed. In Ancient Rome the whole population was involved in a policy of conquest. The Romans, thanks to their warlike superiority, succeeded in making all the countries of the Mediterranean servile to them. The whole population lived on the exploitation of these lands. They became enthusiastic for war, and upheld the most merciless conduct of war; and as success in war brought crowds of cheap slaves to the Romans, it ultimately became one of their pastimes to employ slaves in the amphitheatres, to make them fight one another, and eventually kill each other for the delight of the populace. Gladiatorial contests, and the murdering of men as a mere pastime for an indolent mob of both high and low degree, mark the extreme limit of a most vulgar cruelty; and yet such · facts represent the ancient Roman city, not in the condition of barbarity but at the height of its civilisation. These gladiatorial contests did not cease until the Roman State had been brought down from its high level of " culture," through the incursion of barbarians who were living on the borders.

In the course of economic developments, alongside of the war nobility there developed a capitalist class with two diverging tendencies. Being an exploiter, the capitalist regarded the man, from whose exploitation he lived, not as a means to that man's end, but as a means to his own ends. In such an attitude there lurk already the germs of inhumanity and cruelty, and it depends entirely upon conditions prevailing how far these germs will develop. Colonial policy was responsible for the bloodiest and most fearful atrocities. On the other hand, at the time of commercial monopoly, opposition arose between commercial capital and industrial capital. Commercial capital showed itself to be at this period warlike and unscrupulous. It massacred and plundered the people of India. It carried on slave-driving with negroes, and forced its various governments to embark on murderous and exhausting commercial wars. On the other hand, industrial capital has had to pay the greater part of the costs of these wars, and has been thereby handicapped. It stands, therefore, in direct opposition to such methods, and indeed indignantly so. Human sympathy comes to the surface, and becomes incensed over the treatment of the black slaves in the West Indies, all the while, however, cruelly torturing the white human-beings of England by overwork at starvation wages. But not even the proletariat shows at this stage any consistent and unified tendency. We have seen that the conditions of life forced the proletariat to regard human life as something sacred. Since it is not merely an exploiting, but rather an exploited class, it suffers most from the disregard of human life; so that war imposes upon it, apart from expense, as in the case of Ancient Rome, burdens and dangers; whereas success and the booty derived from war go to the ruling classes alone. All this inspires the proletariat with a horror of all slaughter and of every kind of cruelty. Nevertheless the proletariat does not appear on the historical stage at the same time as the industrial proletariat. Tendencies towards proletarianism appear among the masses long before modern industrial manufacture has become developed through the downfall of feudalism, which imposes upon the peasants heavier taxes so that the peasants' occupation is adversely affected, and the rate of production rapidly sinks.

The result is, that agriculture thus has to turn away more and more labourers, and consequently the burden of labour increases on those who remain behind. Hence at such a time superfluous labour finds little chance of being taken on in industrial occupation, since industry itself is circumscribed by guilds. Therefore countless masses of the unemployed, starving and despairing proletariat swarm the country; and because they themselves are incapable of productive labour, they have recourse to all kinds of parasitical means of livelihood, from begging and stealing to downright robbery. Living in utter misery, excluded from and despised by society, these people are naturally filled with a wild hatred against all society; and the hatred increases, because those in power, incapable and unwilling to take some measures towards social reform, resort to terrorism. The starving people *have* to be checked, by means of frightfulness, from begging, from stealing, from cheating, from prostitution and robbery. The most fearful punishments were thus inflicted on these unfortunate people. "A real bloody war against vagabondage," as Marx described it in his book on "Capital," which gives many examples of this kind of legislation. (Popular edition, pages 664 and following.) The result was the same as that which any reign of terror produces. It lowers social products, without being able to change the ground from whence those products arise. The number of criminals did not diminish, however much they might be sent to the galley-ships, or however much they might be hanged and tortured. For those who survived there remained no other choice than that of leading the life of swindlers Hence arose continual conflict with the police. The only noticeable result was the increasing demoralisation of the proletariat, whose hatred and rage, and whose thirst for blood and cruelty were all increased by the horrors and cruelties of the executions that took place. Of course this was true in the first place only

of the criminal section of the proletariat. This very
section was at that time so numerous, and was connected by so many ties of relationship and comradeship
with the elements of the working-class proletariat, (as
also with the lower strata of the small middle class
as well as of the peasantry, who all stood more or less
with one foot in the bog of evil influences), that even
their own ways of thinking and feeling were affected
by them. As a consequence, all feelings for humanity
were, at the time of the outbreak of the French Revolution, confined to the intellectuals, and to those strata
of the well-to-do sections of the small middle class and
of the capitalists and industrials, who were influenced
by the intellectuals. In the proletariat itself, and in
those strata standing in closest relation with it, the
coarsening and brutalising that resulted from this
bloody legislation often came to the light of day, as
soon as the power of the State, under whose pressure
all this lay hidden, finally broke down.

SLAUGHTER AND TERRORISM.

In view of the treatment meted out to the poorest
elements of the masses by the ruling classes, it is not
to be wondered at that the revolutionary elements, so
soon as they could operate freely, often gave to the
struggle a wild and cruel character, thus turning
the great revolution into one of a particularly sanguinary character. Nevertheless it would be a mistake
to class all revolutionary massacres under one head.
One must moreover distinguish between excesses, to
which a brutalised people, in the passion aroused by
struggle and despair, or out of thoughtless fear, allowed
itself to give way; and those excesses, which are the
result of a pre-considered system of training, and which
are introduced into the State system, in the form of

carefully-planned legislation, by those in power, in order to grind down elements, which seemed to those rulers to be dangerous.

Atrocities which sprang spontaneously from the people we find already at the beginning of the revolution; but the commencement of the Reign of Terror dates from the summer of the year 1793, at the time when the Girondistes were arrested and executed. The people showed their brutality as early as the day of the storming of the Bastille, when the garrison capitulated. Some were killed; others had their heads hacked off, which were triumphantly carried round on pikes. This parading of heads on pikes happened often enough during the course of the revolution. The thirst for blood and cruelty increased when it came to a war of the Revolution with the monarchs of Europe. When the Prussian army was marching on Paris and the Prussian Commander-in-Chief, the Duke of Brunswick, in his manifesto, threatened Paris with total destruction, rumours as to a conspiracy of the aristocrats throughout the land in support of the external enemy were rampant. Then did the Parisians rise in uncontrolled and fearful rage, in order to annihilate the political prisoners in the prisons. That took place on September 2nd, 1792. This massacre, which cost 3,000 men their lives, represented the height of the horrors of the great revolution. A very intoxication for blood seized these crowds of executioners. They were not content with killing. They literally bathed with delirious delight in blood.

The Princess de Lamballe, whose whole crime consisted merely in being a friend of the Queen, was not only killed; but her body was cut open and her heart torn out. Her head was put on a pike, and brought to the imprisoned Queen before the window. At the sight of this horror the Queen swooned away.

Even acts of mercy took on a cruel form. An example may be found in the experience that happened

to Mme. de Sombreuill, who at the time of the
September massacres was in prison with her father.
A certain M. de Saint Mart, who was near her father,
had his skull split open. Her father was to suffer the
same fate; whereupon she in desperation covered him
with her own body, and fought for a long time, until
she succeeded, after having received three wounds, in
moving these men.

"One of them took a glass, poured therein blood
that was flowing from the head of the murdered M. de
Saint Mart, mixed it with wine and powder, and said
that if she would drink that to the health of the nation
she could save her father. She did this without a
shudder, and was forthwith carried out by these self-
same men."

(This report is presented in the collection of "Letters
from the French Revolution," by Gustav Landauer,
2nd volume, page 176, which was finished in the
summer before the latest German Revolution. The
Preface, dated June, 1918, closes with the following
remark: "An intimate knowledge of the spirit and
the tragedy of the Revolution should be of help to us
in the serious times that now confront us." The
unfortunate man little suspected how soon, in these
"serious times," the tragedy of the Revolution would
be fulfilled on his own person.)

There is no doubt that the cruelty of the enraged
and desperate masses in the Revolution was terrible.
But one should not blame the Revolution alone for
that, even if one is justified in ever blaming mental
occurrences of this kind. They were the result of the
treatment that had been meted out to the people
by high authority for many a long day. Just one
example.

In the year 1757 a man, Damiens by name,
attempted the life of Ludwig XV. He attacked him
with a kind of penknife, which proved to be quite
harmless. But the revenge for this deed was terrible.

Damiens' right hand was hacked off, and burnt before his own eyes. Wounds were made in his arms, legs and chest, and boiling oil and molten lead were poured into these wounds. Then they bound each of his limbs to horses, and drove the animals each in different directions, so that his whole body was literally torn to pieces. This infamous torture was executed in full publicity, in order to make an effect on the crowd. The effect, alas, we know.

Such barbarities were perpetrated till right into the time of the Revolution. It was really the Revolution that finally brought them to an end. But still, on August 13th, 1789, Gaultier de Biauzat made the following report from Versailles:

"Last Tuesday, about midday, the people of Versailles succeeded in preventing the execution of a criminal, who had been condemned, on account of patricide, to be bound alive to a wheel and burnt." ("Landauer's Letters." volume 1, page 315.)

"These atrocities committed by those in higher authority preceded those perpetrated by the masses. The slaughter, which the masses engaged in, found no approbation from the acknowledged leaders of the Revolution. Indeed, they inveighed bitterly against such deeds. Such was the case with the September massacres, which have been quite falsely attributed to those leaders. If one could attach any blame to them, it would be, at the very most, that they were unable to restrain the rage of the mob. This rage was so terrible, so fearful and intimidating, that nobody dared to risk falling a victim to it, not even the Girondistes. The Commissioners of the Commune endeavoured, with danger to their own lives, to rescue the ladies in immediate attendance on the Queen; and they succeeded in every case with one exception, that of the Princess de Lamballe, whom we mentioned above." (Kropotkin's "French Revolution," volume 2, page 5.)

Among those who were most incensed over the

September massacres was Robespierre. He cried bitterly, "Blood, ever and always blood. These miserable people will end in drowning the Revolution in
blood." (Louis Blanc, " French Revolution," volume
2, page 207.)

Even Marat himself recoiled horror-stricken before
those massacres. " It is characteristic of Marat himself, a fact which according to my knowledge has
not yet been mentioned by any historian, that he
openly disavowed the September massacres, or at least
bitterly regretted them—the self-same Marat, who
recommended them in his issue of August 19th, and the
benefit of which massacres he, on September 2nd,
wished to extend to the whole of France." (Jean
Jaurès, " La Convention," volume 1, page 75.)

Needless to say, in the case of Marat it was more
political consideration than regard for humanity that
made him disavow the September massacres. Robespierre, on the other hand, belonged to the intellectuals,
who were fundamentally opposed to any shedding of
blood. This he proved in the Constituent Assembly,
in the discussion on May 17th, 1791, over the new penal
law. At the discussion of the new penal law, when
the death penalty came under consideration, Robespierre was among those who most vehemently opposed
this penaltp, on the ground that it did not prevent
crime, but merely made the populace more brutal and
more inclined to deeds of violence. His efforts were
frustrated. The death penalty remained. Only the
most horrible forms of its execution were to be
prohibited. Decapitation only was retained. This
decision formed one of the very rare occasions that
caused Marat to express his approval of the National
Assembly, in opposition to Robespierre. Two years
later Robespierre found himself on Marat's side, and
was obliged to renounce his opposition to the death
penalty. From henceforward this penalty was his

chief political weapon, even against his own political friends.

We have already urged that the well-planned and orderly execution of terrorist methods should not oe classed with the excesses of an excited mob. For these excesses had their origin among the uncultivated and coarse elements of the populace, whereas the Regiment of Terror, was maintained by highly culti-vated men who were filled with the most humane feelings. This Regiment of Terror was the result of the conditions then existent, and was different in origin from the spontaneous atrocities. These latter were a result of the merciless legislation of the old regime against the poverty-stricken masses; whereas the Regiment of Terror was forced on the Jacobins because they, in the most appalling circumstances and in the midst of a war, which had come about through the misery of the decaying masses, and only became paramount when the Jacobins came into power, found themselves face to face with a task that was insoluble. The task they had to solve was to preserve bourgeois society and private property, and at the same time to do away with the misery of the people. The result of this was that they found themselves in a most des-perate position, out of which they could extricate them-selves only by the employment of the very means of which they themselves disapproved, and of whose uselessness they were perfectly well aware. It was the very misery of the masses that caused the old regime to proceed to its bloody legislation, and to have recourse to terrorism. Indeed, the general misery itself gave rise to this bloody legislation, to the terror-ism of the new regime. The only difference was, that the *ancient State* endeavoured to gain the mastery over the wretched populace, by beheading and ill-treating the poor; whereas the *new State* sought to diminish the misery of the masses, by beheading—without ill-treating—the rich and their servants. Yet the one failed of its object just as did the other. But even in this respect there was a difference. The existence of the old regime did not depend upon whether the Regiment of Terror destroyed the proletariat or not. The failure of terrorism was certainly a disagreeable fact, but it represented no serious danger for the old State, because the ·.lass that it wished to keep under, namely, the mob proletariat, was quite incapable, by its own strength, of ever gaining the upper hand, and was, from an economic point of view, a completely negligible factor. The new regime, on the other hand, was bankrupt, and went to pieces as soon as its terrorism failed. For the class that it tried to keep under, namely, the bourgeoisie, was the very one which, under the circumstances, was best calculated to gain the supremacy; and at that time it was, economically considered, indispensable. The repression of this bourgeois class hindered social development and production, and in consequence gave rise to still greater misery, even among the very people who should have derived advantage from the Reign of Terror. And a still greater difference distinguishes the old from the new "Reign of Terror." In the case of the former, it corresponded entirely with the ethics of the circles that directed it. They were not necessarily unfaithful to themselves, by putting terrorism into practice. It appeared to them to ne a perfectly obvious and justifiable means. The new Reign of Terror, however, was set up in absolute opposition to the ethics of the class that put it into execution. From the very beginning, therefore, the terrorists suffered from a bad conscience, which they endeavoured to salve by all sorts of sophistry, but which nevertheless undermined their moral strength, lessened their authority, and increased the friction and the insecurity then existing, and even rendered corrupt many of their members. Even if there be no absolute "morale" existing in the world beyond, and even supposing that the morality of a particular time, of a particular country, or of a particular class, is something relative, ethics do remain the strongest social bond, and the stoutest support in all problems and conflicts of life. Nothing can be worse than unfaithfulness to oneself, or to act against those ethical principles that one has acknowledged as forming the categorical imperative. It was the result of all this which contributed largely to the complete destruction of the Reign of Terror, as soon as it met with energetic opposition. How quickly the surviving terrorists became converted to quite other views! The legitimate Monarchists were for Napoleon a far greater danger than the old Republicans. This was proof of how seriously the " morale " of these latter had suffered in the Reign of Terror.

The Humanising of Conduct in the Nineteenth Century.

The great French Revolution belongs to the most sanguinary epoch of world history, and many people have drawn the conclusion that the shedding of blood is one of the indispensable factors in a real revolution. In consequence they have either condemned the Revolution or glorified slaughter. As a matter of fact, the Revolution of 1789 itself removed some of the most important features which gave the Revolution so cruel and violent a character, and prepared the way for milder forms of future revolutions. It accomplished this, on the one hand, by putting aside feudalism and by encouraging industrial capital, which had the effect of turning the masses of the proletariat from being mere vagabonds into wage-earners; and, on the other hand, by starting a movement, which sooner or later was to end with the triumph of democracy. And finally, out of the study of the Revolution, as also of capitalism, a theory arose which enabled the proletarian party, in every given moment, to take some practical action, the object of which lay within the bounds of possibility; so that there was no reason for it to fall into one of those blind alleys, which would only lead to a Reign of Terror. Through the Revolution the peasant was emancipated, and became master of his own land. As a result, land economy reached a higher stage and produced greater returns, of which the peasants had the benefit; and therefore there was a decrease in the amount of superfluous labour that had abandoned agricultural work. On the other hand, there was a great incursion of men coming from the land, who were now seeking employment in the town. All the old guild restrictions had broken down; manual labour could develop itself unimpeded. It is true that, in one way after the other, such labour was adversely affected by the rising industrial capital; but even this helped to develop, with its rapid increase, large demands for labour. The industrial proletariat now became a special class with a special class-consciousness, which became more and more pronounced, and differed from the mob proletariat.

Under capital the position of the industrial proletariat had certainly deteriorated, in comparison with that of the independent labourer at the time when manual labour was prosperous. On the other hand, capital certainly improved the position of labour as against the mob proletariat. A mob proletariat is, as a class, incapable of struggle; whereas the industrial proletariat, by its class struggles and by its organisation obtained a marvellous result and a remarkable intellectual and moral impetus. In the very beginning the industrial proletariat was dreadfully kept under by capital, not only economically, but also morally so. In its housing conditions, in the meagreness and uncertainty of its existence, in its ignorance, it was not far removed from the mob proletariat. Indeed, it stood in many respects below it on account of the monotony of its life, as a result of the continuous oppression of factory discipline, which excluded all liberty of action, through the callous sweating of women and children.

As a result, the boldness of the more powerful elements of the mob proletariat was absent from the working proletariat. Hence it became less sensitive, but it did not thereby get rid of its coarseness. In such a condition it would have been quite impossible to think of emancipation. Only after a long time could a man, by engaging in continuous class struggle, expect to extricate himself from the seemingly hopeless bog that threatened to engulf him. The more this process went on, the more were the tendencies towards humanisation, which came to light as the result of the conditions then prevailing, able to develop and grow. Favourable to these tendencies was the fact that, as a result of the Revolution and of its consequences, even the penal laws erected against the proletariat began to lose the cruel character that they had had before.

These are all the causes of the results which we have already notified, namely, that the revolutionary elements of the proletariat show themselves to have been a class filled with the greatest humanising force, especially in the movement that took place in the nineteenth century; and that they departed more and more from the brutal savagery that distinguished their forerunners at the time of the great French Revolution, and which even Engels observed in the early 'forties of the nineteenth century among the factory hands of England. At the same time, the causes that led to the Reign of Terror disappeared. Already after the collapse of this Reign of Terror, the more far-seeing friends of the proletariat clearly recognised that it could not lead to any emancipation based on bourgeois society. They came to the conclusion that this

object could be achieved only by the doing away with
private property, in respect to the means of production,
and by the introduction of communal production. But
they found neither the necessary material conditions
among the capitalists, nor the psychical conditions
among the proletariat; and they could not see that
economical development and class struggle were at
work to produce these conditions. Therefore, they
endeavoured to solve the social question, and
attempted to find a plan or formula which seemed
possible of practical application, as soon as the necessary means were at their disposal. If the revolutionary
proletariat accepted this idea and sought for power, not
in some philanthropic millionaire, but in the political
dictatorship after the pattern of the first Paris Commune, every such attempt, when undertaken by a
minority in the State, was of necessity bound to lead
to a reign of terror similar to the rule of the first Paris
Commune. In any case this attempt was at least
rational. It did not seek any more to escape the consequences of bourgeois society and yet preserve this
society, but it attempted to remove the consequences
by destroying their foundation. But even this
endeavour must have come to grief when an attempt
was made to put this into practice, so long as the social
conditions failed, which alone could remove the foundations they were attempting to destroy. It would
have meant the attempt of a minority to impose upon
a majority something that was impossible, or at least
without purpose and even contrary to its interests. And
that would have been possible only by resorting to
means of force, which would have culminated in the
necessity for terrorising by means of slaughter.

Such an attempt was frustrated, not only because the
mass of labour at the time was only gradually adopt-
ing social ideas, but because the proletariat for many
decades had no longer maintained so supreme a
position as it had held in conjunction with those

elements of the small bourgeoisie in Paris, with which it had been in close contact from 1789 to 1794. The second Paris Commune indeed gave it authority over Paris, but not over France; and even in Paris the Socialists were not in the majority. In fact, these latter had no sure theoretical foundation, and therefore they were very cautious and retiring. They found a much stronger basis after the Commune, when Marxism began to be accepted by the masses. It was the conception that Marx and Engels had given in the 'forties, and had deepened and extended in the 'fifties and 'sixties; in other words, it was the materialistic conception of history. They embodied the idea of a perfectly natural development in history, which, according to their ideas, was governed by the development of economical relations.   From this standpoint they realised that the capitalist means of production resulted in conditions that ultimately made necessary and inevitable a socialist means of production; but they equally well recognised the fruitlessness of any attempt to replace the first method of production by the second, so long as the conditions were not ripe for that.

For these men, therefore, the task of the Socialists lay no more in finding a plan or a formula for general socialisation, which should forward and, in all conditions, introduce Socialism. They had to study economic conditions, and as a result of their studies, make clear what was necessary for society in general, and endeavour to fight for its introduction.   In other words, the Socialists from now onwards were not merely concerned in introducing Socialism.   Where this was not yet possible, they were forced to concern themselves with the conditions of capitalist industry, and demand their development in proletarian interests. But this was by no means immediately understood by the Socialists themselves.   Indeed, even in the International, some years later, the Socialists

regarded with contempt such matters as free trade and
the strike, because such things did not affect the
system of wages. It was Marx and Engels who taught
the workers the importance of the proletarian struggle
for emancipation, of the economic problems and conflicts of the capitalist system of that time. Socialism
for the proletariat schooled in Marxist thought thus
ceased to be something that could at once be introduced and realised everywhere, and under any conditions. Even where it did obtain political power, it
had to introduce only so much of Socialism as was
possible under the existing conditions, and in a
form corresponding to those particular conditions.
According to this conception, Socialism could not be
introduced by means of a *coúp d' état*. It was to be
the result of a long historical process. At the same
time, the Socialists were for ever being urged to undertake, in any given moment, only what was possible
under the conditions, material and moral, then prevailing. If, therefore, everything was to be done with due
consideration it would have been impossible for the
Socialists to fail of anything they undertook, or for
them to find themselves in a desperate condition, which
should force them to act contrary to the spirit of the
proletariat and of Socialism, and have recourse to
Terrorism.

In fact, since Marxism has led the Socialist movement, this latter, even up to the beginning of the great
world war, has in nearly every one of its actions always
been preserved from grave defects, and the idea of
carrying anything out by means of Terrorism has completely dropped out of its programme. Much contributed to this result. At the same time in which
Marxism became the dominant social doctrine, democracy had taken root in Western Europe, and had
begun, as a result of its struggles there, to form a sound
foundation for political life. In consequence of this,
not only were the enlightenment and organisation of

the proletariat facilitated, but also its insight into economic conditions as well as into the relative power of the classes increased. Hence all fantastic adventures were eliminated, as also was civil war, as a means of class struggle. In 1902 I wrote in my pamphlet "The Social Revolution" (chapter 6, "Democracy"):

"Democracy is one of the highest values, if for no other reason than because it makes possible higher forms of revolutionary struggle. This struggle will no longer be like that of 1789 or 1848, a struggle of unorganised masses without any political education, or without any insight into the relative powers of the' struggling elements, and without any deeper understanding of the objects of the struggle and the means for its solution. It will be no longer a struggle of masses that let themselves be carried away by every rumour, and by every chance circumstance. It will be a struggle of organised enlightened masses, full of stability and reflection, who do not follow on every impulse, who do not explode over every disadvantage, and who do not become downhearted as the result of failure. On the other hand, election and the means thereto make it possible to take stock of oneself and of one's enemies. They help towards a clear insight into the relative strength of the classes and parties. Further, they put a check on over-hasty action, and overcome defeat. They also help to make even the opponent himself recognise the untenable nature of his position, and often cause him voluntarily to abandon it, wherever such might prove to be a matter of life and death for him. Thus all struggle becomes less cruel and merciless, unless dependent on blind chance."

As a result of the combined working of all these conditions, of the formation of the industrial proletariat, and of the elevation of this latter above the level of the mob proletariat; as a result, further, of the development of Socialist theory and the establishment of democracy, it was possible to put in the background the gloomy fears, which Engels even in 1845 expressed in his book, "The Position of the Working-Classes in England," where he said:—

" If the English middle-class does not reflect—and it seems to have no intention of doing so—there will follow a revolution, which will bear no comparison with any that has hitherto taken place. The proletariat, driven to despair, will seize their torches. The revenge of the people will betray such rage, of which not even the year 1793 can give us any idea. The war of the poor against the rich will be the most fearful that has ever been waged." (2nd Edition, page 298.)

It must be said that Engels' fears would have been justified only in the case of a revolution breaking out at the time he expected. Even in the 'forties his fears were still rather exaggerated, in spite of the fact that crowds of undeveloped people, especially Irish, had been engaged in industry. But Engels himself expected that, if the revolution would not come soon, the proletariat would have time to develop itself, and become imbued with a Socialist spirit, which would then cause the revolution to take some milder form.

" In proportion as the proletariat assimilates Socialist and Communist elements, will the shedding of blood, vengeance and rage decrease in the revolution." The revolution expected by Engels came in 1848, but not in England. After the outbreak there began in all countries in Europe an epoch of capitalist development, which was accompanied by a growth of the economic, intellectual, and moral strength of the working-classes.

In the most progressive countries of Europe things rapidly changed. As early as 1872, a year after the Commune, Marx gave expression to the hope that, in countries like America, England and Holland, the proletariat would assume a peaceful form. Ever since that time, the rise of the proletariat has brought with it further progress. Yet no one with a keen insight into the matter can suppose that a monarchy based on militarism, such as the German, Austrian and Russian, can be overturned by means of force alone. But, even in this matter, people thought less of slaughter by actual weapons, and more and more of the one means best suited to the proletariat for obtaining its object, namely, refusal to work, or, in other words, the *strike*. It was perfectly clear that the men of the old regime in Germany, as also in Russia, would endeavour to crush any attempt to overthrow them by a resort to arms. But that a considerable section of the proletariat, when once it came to power, should again have recourse to slaughter, revenge and rage, as did indeed happen at the end of the eighteenth century, was expected by no one. This set the whole development upside down.

In opposition to the views of Engels, who was the author of the book " The Development of Socialism from Utopia to Knowledge," which voiced the belief that there would be a continuous diminution of barbarity and cruelty in future proletarian revolutions, another view has lately been discussed in a book entitled " The Development of Socialism from Knowledge to Action," which appears in the preface to a book entitled " The Programme of the Communists," by N. Bucharin (Zurich, 1918). There it is written:—

" The more capitalism develops in any country, the more reckless will be its defenceless struggle, and so the more murderous will be the *proletarian revolution,* the more cruel the measures by means of which the victorious working-class will tread under foot the defeated capitalists " (page 19).

This is the very contrary to what Marx and Engels had expected It is all the more wrong, since it erects into a general law for the whole of social development those Bolshevik practices that have prevailed for the last eighteen months. It is wrong, because it declares these practices to be the outcome of the recklessness and the brutality of the capitalists' defenceless war. Of all this brutality there was no sign in November, 1917, in Petersburg and in Moscow; and still less recently in Budapest. But that the proletarian revolution has become more murderous in the extreme is perfectly true. The reason for this state of affairs, I, in my "senile obstinacy" or my "senile stupidity" (Bucharin, page 22), attribute, in any case, to other factors than capitalist barbarity, which was never less evident in the countries involved in the world-war than in Germany at the beginning of the last revolution.

THE EFFECTS OF THE WAR.

The real cause of the change, in the process of the hitherto recorded development towards humanisation, into a development towards brutality is attributable to the world-war; but even earlier there were other factors that were inimical to the general tendency of the humanising influence. The most important of these was brought to light by the very French Revolution itself. It was *universal military service*, which the revolutionary regime found necessary, in order, by means of a superiority of troops and the continual filling up of vacant appointments, to cope with the professional armies of the united monarchs arraigned against them. There was only one of these monarchic States, which introduced this system and indeed preserved and developed it at a time when France had already again discarded it. This was *Prussia*, the smallest and most recent of the great Powers of Europe, with the most unfavourable frontiers; whose very existence demanded an army, which, in relation to the population, was far greater than that in any other land. Apart from this fact, the old Prussia, from perfectly natural causes, was regarded as a stepchild and the poorest among the great States. If, therefore, it really wished to assert itself, all other considerations had to go in favour of the army. As a consequence, ever since the day of its ascendancy, when it ranked as one of the great Powers, it has been a militarist State *par excellence*. In his book on Germany (" My Four Years in Germany," London, 1917, page 447) Gerard, the American Ambassador, makes several remarks, which show up Prussia's military calling in a drastic light.

Thanks to universal military service and the upholding of militarism in general, Prussia arrived at the height of its power in the West, between 1866 and 1870. As a result, universal service was forced upon the remaining States of the European Continent, and at about the same time the railway system became a decisive factor in the conduct of war. All military States endeavoured to develop this system to the best of their powers, which brought about the necessity for a continuous increase of armed force—in other words, a more and more rigid application of universal service. Hence we finally arrived at the glorious result, that the whole of the male population, which was not crippled or physically unfit, was pressed into war service! But war service means the becoming accustomed to the shedding of human blood, and to competition in such shedding. It signifies the deadening of human feelings, of culture, and the cultivation of brutality. In the eighteenth century, when there were only small professional armies (militia), the great mass of the people was preserved from such influences on their morals; but, as a consequence of universal military service, the people, in the course of the nineteenth century, became more and more brutalised, and first and foremost in Prussia.

The humanising tendencies of the nineteenth century were thereby not wholly without effect; but they were most adversely affected. These humanising tendencies became most pronounced in the case of the intellectual elements. These remained longest exempt from military service, even at the time when, instead of voluntary enlistment, forced recruiting was resorted to. But, under the conscription system, it was in the first place only the peasants, artisans, and the labour classes, who were affected; the middle class and the intellectuals were spared. Universal service, however, could ultimately make no exception in their case. On the contrary, officers to command reserves were required. But before, as after, the educated man occupied a special position in regard to military service. It was not a position that excluded him from the army, but one in which he, within the army itself, as a volunteer for one year and as a reserve officer, had certain privileges. As a result, the educated classes had the influences of military force on their thoughts and feelings, and indeed to a still higher degree than was the case with the other classes. For it put them in a privileged position and created in them already a certain taste for army life. Moreover, the system of professional officers enhanced the attraction of the army. Those who had made military service their life vocation, for whom it was no mere temporary form of activity, and who in all war measures had to take the initiative, and make their regiment excel in energy and smartness, developed the characteristic traits of militarism; in a still higher degree than the ordinary men, who had to serve for only a short period, and even then were compelled to do so.

As a result, the educated classes were more strongly influenced by militarism than even the rest of the population. Furthermore, professional occupation brings with it a tendency to develop every idea and conception in a more thorough and radical way—which after all is quite compatible with very reactionary modes of thought—than is the case with men, who, through practical experience, know the obstacles that occur in daily life. Those of the educated classes who wished to become reserve officers, and took as their example the professional officers, easily adapted themselves to militarism, and became the very pioneers of roughness and violence which, the outcome of universal service, soon spread to the whole of the people. Even in this respect Prussia was to the forefront of the other States; since it first introduced the system of one year volunteers and reserve officers, and raised the reserve officer, more than any other State had done, to a privileged and much-coveted position. Yet, in spite of universal military service, the humanising tendencies in the proletariat were stronger, as a result of its class position, than the brutalising influence of militarism. In the case of the educated classes, especially in Prussia, a strong check was put on these tendencies, which contributed not a little to the bitterness of class opposition and class struggle.

What is here said of the educated applies especially to the capitalists, whose humane instincts, from the outset, find stronger opposing forces to overcome, as a result of their position. When, therefore, the war broke out and dragged in its train for four years practically the whole of the healthy male population, the coarsening tendencies of militarism sank to the very depths of brutality, and lack of human feeling and sentiment. Even the proletariat could no longer escape from its influence. It was in a very high degree infected by militarism, and when it returned home again, was in every way brutalised. Habituated to war, the man who had come back from the front was only too often in a state of mind and feeling that made him ready, even in peace times and among his own people, to enforce his claims and interests by deeds of violence and bloodshed. That became, as it were, an element of the civil war; it also contributed further to make the masses mere savages. Nevertheless, many of the more mature, as soon as they were removed from the influences of war, fell easily enough into the ways of thinking and feeling they had acquired in times of peace. It is much worse, however, in the case of youths; for they, without any teachers or guides, have been powerless to withstand the brutalising influences that prevailed during the four years of the war; and hence have received impressions, which they can never eradicate completely, so long as they lived.

Besides all this, there is a very profound change at work in the very conditions of the proletariat. The war has affected most seriously the small middle class, and has claimed many of their ranks, and forced them into the proletariat. Moreover, these elements, who hitherto remained aloof from all proletarian class struggles, have not come into contact with the discipline and the capacity for organisation, which the proletariat had acquired at the time when the class struggle was under the leadership of the Socialist Parties. These took the trouble to enlighten and organise the masses; and even within the proletariat, as it has been hitherto constituted, there have been very profound changes. As was the case with all workers, the reduction in number of the skilled workers in time of war, through death, or through injury and sickness, had become much greater than in times of peace.

At the same time, hardly any provision was made for the rising generation. There was no time or strength to educate the young, and there was also lacking the very need to undertake such activity. Instead of the varied industries that existed in times of peace, there rose up the much more monotonous war industry, which offered only small scope for skilled labour; and each labourer had only to learn the use of a little machinery, which most unskilled apprentices could manipulate just as well. In consequence, the number of skilled labourers, who have contributed so enormously to Germany's industrial development, became very greatly reduced during the war; and in their stead there has sprung up unskilled labour, the numbers of which have rapidly increased. The skilled labourers were the best organised and best educated, and were the clearest thinking of all the labour classes. The unskilled were unorganised, ignorant and indifferent. Their indifference certainly disappeared during the war. For this gigantic event, with its fearful consequences, roused everyone, even the most remote elements of the people, and brought them to the most feverish excitement. At the same time, however, the number of skilled workers, brought up on Socialist doctrine, diminished, as against the numbers of those who, in every respect, were ignorant and undisciplined; and also as against the increase of the small middle class, which had been forced into the proletariat. As a result, the minority with superior education and skill, who had hitherto led the proletariat, gradually lost its power of leading, and in its stead there arose the blind passion of ignorance. This became all the more easy, because the war brought in its train the most profound economic chaos, a huge amount of unemployment, an enormous increase in high prices, and lack of the necessaries of life. So the desperate masses demanded the most radical changes; not indeed in order to create a newer and higher form of society about which they, as a matter of fact, had not given a thought, but in order to escape immediately from their horrible misery. For the proletariat the change of its wretched situation is always an urgent matter. That is the chief reason why, since considerable economic and historical knowledge is a necessary requisite for the understanding of Marxism, Marx's mode of thought has never found it easy to take root among the labouring classes. The masses do not instinctively prefer a doctrine which leads towards the road of development, but one which offers a formula or a plan, the carrying out of which will inevitably

relieve them, in all circumstances, from the suffering
they have to endure. For a proletarian it argues a
certain amount of resignation on his part to acknowledge a doctrine, which certainly does not expect of
him a state of mere passive waiting, but on the other
hand spurs him on to an energetic continuation of the
class struggle; yet which nevertheless makes his
ultimate emancipation from conditions dependent on
a mode of development, which has first of all to be discovered and created. However difficult it was for the
proletarian in the latter decades before the war, his
position was such that he could, to a certain extent,
live in such a way, that the immediate transformation
of society was for him not a question of life or death;
at least not for the skilled labourer, who formed the
nucleus of the class struggle and of the Socialist movement. Nowadays these workmen are ousted in all
political and economic struggles by the unskilled, and
the conditions for these latter are so desperate that
they cannot afford to wait. Why indeed should they
wait, when the conclusion of the war has finally put the
political power into their hands?

The war has not only brought the most solid elements
of the working-classes into the forefront of the class
struggle; but it has also, as the result of the collapse
of the armies, especially in those parts of Europe which
are economically most solid, created the proletariat
class in the various towns, by the side of which illiterate
peasants, such as are to be found in Russia, have not
been able to acquire any real independent political
power. No class ever voluntarily renounces the power
that it has won for itself, whatever be the circumstances that have brought it to the fore. It would
be folly to demand of the Russian and Hungarian
proletariats such renunciation, on account of the backward state of their countries. But a Socialist Party
led by a truly Marxist spirit would adapt the present
problems confronting the victorious proletariat to the

material and psychical conditions to be found ready to
hand; and would not endeavour, without further reflection, to introduce an immediate and complete socialisation in a land of undeveloped capitalist production
like Russia.

Certainly it is questionable whether such a party
could ever lead the masses. To the practical politicians
it seems more important to rule at the moment, than
to run the danger of an economic failure, with a view
to being ultimately in the right. The practical
politician does not like being in a position of inviting
unpopularity at the present moment, because the inevitable collapse of a policy, which exceeds the bounds
of possibility, has been made clear. He prefers to avoid
the collapse, and to preserve his ideal from being com-
promised. The old antagonism between practical
politics and theoretical politics, between Lassalle and
Marx, rose again after the revolution in Russia in 1917.
Marx declared in his letter to Kugelmann, of the 23rd
February, 1865 (published by me in the "Socialist,"
1st May, 1918), that the German working men, as a
result of the reaction of 1849-1859, had become too
much hampered in their development not to "become
jubilant when a deliverer, in the form of a mob orator
like Lassalle, comes and promises to help them at one
move to enter the promised land." Such "moves" and
such "deliverers" were not to Marx's taste. But, as
at the time of Lassalle, the time of the Second Russian
Revolution, if for quite other reasons, proved to be
very unfavourable to Marxist doctrines. Those among
the labouring classes in Russia, who had been trained
on Marxist lines, were dead or swept away by the backward masses, who had suddenly awakened to life. It
was pre-Marxist ways of thought that gained the upper
hand, ways such as were represented by Blanqui,
Weitling or Bakunin. These were the conditions under
which the Revolution, first of all in Russia and then
in the neighbouring countries, progressed. No wonder,

therefore, that it awoke afresh only primitive ways of thought; and also allowed brutal and murderous forms of political and social war to come to light, forms which one had been led to believe had been overcome by the intellectual and moral rise of the proletariat.

CHAPTER VIII.

THE COMMUNISTS AT WORK.

EXPROPRIATION AND ORGANISATION.

The world-war made the working class take a backward step both morally and intellectually. It brutalised almost every strata of the population; it set the most undeveloped elements of the proletariat in the forefront of the movement, and finally increased the necessitous state of the proletariat to such an extent, that it brought despair in the place of quiet thought and reflection. The war also encouraged primitive ideas in the working-classes, by developing the military way of thinking, that form of thinking which, as it is, lies very near the surface in the thoughts of the average unintelligent man, who imagines that mere power is the determining factor in the world history—as if one needed only the necessary force and recklessness to accomplish everything that one undertakes. Marx and Engels have always attacked and opposed this conception. In Engels' classical book ("Herr Eugen Dühring's Transformation of Science") there are three chapters dealing exclusively with "theory of power" (3rd edition, pages 162-192). This theory, from beginning to end, is anti-Marxist. Engels did not hesitate to oppose it wherever it appeared in a revolutionary form. He was not of the view, so much upheld to-day, that one should never show up the mistakes of a movement, if it is a revolutionary proletarian movement, because one might, by so doing, weaken the force of the revolution. Obviously enough, one should not be too strict in judgment on the faults and follies in a revolution. The most difficult historical situation is that of a revolution, in which one stands face to face with a completely new situation, which it is impossible to survey. It would be the very cheapest form of Pharisaism for an observer, himself in a secure position, or regarding from afar, to blame too heavily the mistakes that are made by men who are in the centre of the fight, and who have to bear all its burdens and dangers. But on the other hand, it is absolutely necessary to blame mistakes that do not arise from conceivably false or insufficient information, but which proceed from an inherently false fundamental conception of things. They can be avoided only by overcoming such a conception; and they threaten every future revolutionary movement, if one allows them to pass uncriticised, or even defends them, and glorifies them in the supposed interests of the revolution.

Marx and Engels did not allow themselves to be hindered in such necessary criticism of the revolution, through their " volcanic temperament." This is proved by the criticism that Engels published in the *Leipsig Volkstaat*, in the autumn of 1873. The insurrection, which broke out after the proclamation of the Republic in Spain on the 5th July of that year, was, as early as the 26th January, practically defeated, with some few exceptions, the Carthaginians prolonging the insurrection up to January 8, 1874. Thus, even before the rising was completely quelled, Engels published a very sharp criticism against " this absolutely shameful insurrection . . . which should be a warning to the rest of the world."

This criticism appeared in the series of articles on " The Bakunists at Work " (*Volkstaat*, 31st October, 2nd and 5th November), newly-printed, 1894, in the magazine *Internationales aus dem Volkstaat*, by Freiderich Engels (Berlin *Vorwärts* edition).

We recommend this work to the study of all who are busying themselves with Bolshevism. For Bolshevism is, in many respects, foreshadowed in that

work, since the situation of the Spanish Revolution
bears many analogies to that of the Commune of the
present day. Engels began with a reference to the
fact that, in Spain, the Internationalists in their
majority belonged to the Bakunist Alliance, and he
continues:

" When, in February, 1873, the Republic was proclaimed, the Spanish Alliancists were in a very difficult position. Spain is a land so very backward in
industry that, in that country, it is quite impossible
to speak of an immediate and complete emancipation
of the working classes. Before this is possible, Spain
must pass through several preliminary stages on the
road to development, and clear out of the way a vast
number of obstacles. The Republic gave opportunity
for the country to pass through these preliminary
stages in the shortest possible period, and to remove
the hindrances as soon as possible. But this occasion
could only be put to any use through actual political
participation on the part of the Spanish working-
classes." (Pages 17 and 18).

That would, however, have meant to participate in
the voting for the Cortès and the National Assembly,
and to have taken active part in the same. But the
Bakunists wanted the immediate and complete
emancipation of the working-classes. As a means to
this purpose, the parliamentary democracy, considering the then state of affairs in Spain, was absolutely
incapable, however necessary it was as a means towards the development and the maturing of the proletariat. Participation in " any kind of vote appeared
to them to be crime worthy of death."

Now what did they want to put in the place of an
election campaign? The working-men's council, as a
means for the " immediate and complete emancipation
of the working-classes," had not yet been discovered.
The Bakunists proclaimed a *general strike*, and the
dividing up of Spain into numberless small cantons;

along with, from the very start, the splitting up of
the whole movement into a series of local movements,
and the declaration of the revolution. The end of the
story was not merely the collapse of the movement,
the ruin of the Spanish Internationale, but also " the
abnegation of the principles hitherto preached by the
Bakunists " (page 32), which they had to give up, one
after the other, as a result of the force of circumstances.

Is it any different in Russia to-day? It is true that,
at the outbreak of the present revolution among the
working classes of Russia, it was Marxism and not
anarchy that was reigning.   As a Socialistic theory,
Marxism has never received such general recognition
as in Russia.

For decades the Russian Socialists had made a
virtue out of necessity, and espied in the backward
character   of   their   agrarian   problems   a   certain
advantage. They thought that what there was of the
village communism, in regard to land, made it particularly easy for them to establish and build up modern
Socialism. It was the great service of the Marxists
in Russia, led by Axelrod and Plechanoff, to fight for
recognition of this conception, and by a long and weary
struggle to succeed, in view of the undeveloped state
of the Russian proletariat and of Russian society in
general, in making the inevitable revolution from the
outset take on only a bourgeois character, even if the
proletariat was called upon to play a prominent part
in it.   This view was triumphant in the Russian
Socialist movement, so long as the Revolution did not
bring the proletariat into power, which had for its programme the problem of immediate emancipation; and
also so long as Socialism was professed by the intellectuals and a certain high level of the working-classes.
Consistent Marxism was thrown into a very difficult
position when the Revolution set in motion the really
great mass of the Russian people, who were conscious

G

only of their needs and desires, and who did not care at all whether what they desired was, under the then circumstances, possible and socially advantageous. In the case of the Bolsheviks, Marxism had no power on the situation. The mass psychology overruled them, and they allowed themselves to be carried away by it. Doubtless in consequence of this they have become the rulers of Russia. It is quite another question what will and must be the end of it all. By making the blind will of the masses the motive force of the Revolution, they threw overboard the Marxist system, to the victorious ascendancy of which they had, in a large measure, contributed. With their scientific knowledge, and as the result of the popularity of Marx's name, they thought they had settled everything by taking a Marxist motto, the motto of " the dictatorship of the proletariat." With these words they hoped to gain absolution from all sins against the spirit of Marxism.

The Revolution came as a result of the war. The soldiers were tired of it and would no longer fight. The Bolsheviks made themselves the most formidable representatives of the disinclination to continue the war. They insisted on the dissolution of the army by every means in their power, caring not a bit whether this should be favourable to the German military autocracy or not. If this military autocracy did not win, and it came to a German Revolution, the Bolsheviks were certainly not responsible for that.

The complete collapse of the army gave complete freedom to the lower classes. The peasants immediately insisted on confiscating the landed property, and dividing it up into private property. It was impossible to avoid these large estates being given over to the peasantry, but the problem should have been tackled in such a way, that the technical advantages obtained from these estates should not be lost. But that would have required time, and besides, the peasants would not wait.

The Bolsheviks won the peasants over to their side, by introducing anarchy in the country, and by allowing every community to have a free hand; so that the destruction of these estates went on in the most primitive fashion, with technical loss and the destruction of many means of production. In return, however, the peasants allowed the Bolsheviks a completely free hand in the towns in which they had already likewise won over the working classes; so that these latter were obedient merely to the Bolsheviks' will, and took no regard for the actual conditions of things.

The proletariat was starving. It felt itself repressed and exploited, so it demanded with increasing energy the immediate throwing off of the capitalist yoke. To satisfy its will there was no time for study or reflection. With a few heavy blows the whole edifice of Russian capitalism lay in ruins. The substitution of Socialism for capitalism embraces two questions— one of *property*, and the other of *organisation*. It claims the abolition of private property in regard to means of production, and the transformation of social property in the form of a State and communistic property. It also claims the substitution of a socialistic in place of a capitalistic organisation of the management and of all such functions in one complete economic whole. Of these two transformations, that concerned with property is more simple. Nothing is easier than to expropriate a capitalist. That is a mere question of force, and not necessarily to be connected with any social theory. Long before there was such a thing as industrial capitalism, at the time, namely, of mere commercial and monied capital, we find similar expropriation of merchants, bankers and money-lenders, through the feudal lords and princes, and indeed through the people themselves. In the Middle Ages, not only were the Jews often expropriated; but despite the piety of the time, from time to time also the treasury of a church, or of a particular order would be confiscated.   For instance, Philip IV. of France, at the beginning of the fourteenth century, expropriated the enormously wealthy order of the Knights of the Temple.   Long before there was such a thing as modern Socialism, many good, naïve people often regarded the noble robbers, who despoiled the rich in order to give to the poor, as benefactors of the human race.   To carry out this form of Socialism was easy enough.   It was in keeping with the undeveloped state of the Russian proletariat that Bakunin, in 1864, immediately before the war and the Commune, in his manifesto to the Russian youth of the time, pointed to the way taken by the Russian robber-captain, Stenka Rasin, who in 1667 formed a band of robbers, with whom he lived four whole years in South Russia, until the Government overpowered and killed him.

It is not so easy to organise as it is to expropriate. A capitalist concern is a complex organisation, which finds its intelligence in the capitalist himself, or in his representative.   If it is desired to abolish capitalism, some form of organisation must be created, which should be possible of functioning as well, if not better, without the capitalist head.   This is not so simple as was the procedure of Philip IV. or of Stenka Razin; for it demands a certain set of conditions of a material as well as of a psychical order, a high development of capitalistic organisation, not only of production but also of the export and import of raw materials. Moreover, it also demands a proletariat, which is conscious of its duties, not only towards its own neighbours and comrades, but also towards society as a whole—a proletariat, moreover, which has become accustomed to voluntary discipline and self-administration through long years of mass organisation; and which, finally, is intelligent enough to distinguish the possible from the impossible, and the scientifically educated leader with character from an ignorant demigod without a conscience. Wherever these conditions are not present, capitalism cannot with any success be permanently dissolved by Socialism. And even in those districts, and in those branches of industry in which these conditions are already sufficiently highly developed, the Socialistic organisation must be carefully prepared by a profound examination of the actual conditions. For the forms which the new organisations have, for the time being, taken on are not necessarily the best for all branches of industry, for all lands and all times. They are not " ready-made Utopias " or eternal " ideals." Under certain circumstances they can differ a good deal, and must be adapted according to the prevailing conditions in the most business-like manner possible, if they are to have any success.

But both factors in socialisation, that is, expropriation and reorganisation, must remain in closest connection, if chaos and an absolute standstill are not to follow on the state of production that has hitherto existed. Philip IV. or Stenka Razin could confine their activities to mere expropriation, for they had no intention of creating some new method of production. The transition to Socialism is not possible by this simple means. The masses were impatient. They would not wait. In order to appease them the Bolsheviks, when they came into power, cut the socialising process into two parts. They separated its factors one from the other, although the one without the other cannot live. They proceeded at first after Stenka Razin's approved method, afterwards endeavouring to proceed with organisation as well as it would go. The two things that were intimately connected with one another, and could only work in conjunction, were separated and torn asunder. Lenin himself acknowledged this in April, 1918, in his book, " The immediate problems of the Soviet Power."

" Up to the present, the first consideration was to find measures for an immediate expropriation of the expropriators.   Now the first thing to be done is to organise the finance and control of all business concerns, in which the capitalists have already been expropriated, as well as in all other concerns '' (page 14).

" Our work, which we have to accomplish with the aid of the proletariat, which consists in the organisation of the general financing, and control over the production and the distribution of material products, has been behind our efforts to secure the immediate expropriation of profiteers.   In regard to the socialistic transformation in these departments (and they are very important and essential departments), we have been very backward; and we have remained backward for the very good reason that the financing and control have been far too little organised '' (page 23).

Business concerns and branches of industry were expropriated without any attempt being made to discover whether their organisation on Socialist lines was possible. Even in such departments, where such organisation would have been possible, they were quite content, in the first place, with expropriation; because this alone was possible to carry out without preparation, and also because the working classes would not wait. But the consequences very soon showed themselves. Economic life in Russia is backward owing to the fact that its industry, in comparison with its agricultural life, employs but a very small section of the population; but inside this industry the most modern and up-to-date forms of large manufacture predominate. They had far surpassed the state of Parisian industry of 1871. For in this latter, in so far as anything can be said about socialisation at all, the form of productive associations alone came into question.

The Russian factories were for the most part large concerns, and therefore the first thing that appeared necessary to be done, after the abolition of capital, seemed to be their nationalisation. In productive associations the wages of the labourer depend on his work and on his associates. The scale of these wages is determined by the number of products that are brought to market. They themselves must look after the buying and selling of raw materials. In the nationalised factories the workmen drew their money no more from the capitalists, as they had done before, but from the State. The maximum of their wages depended much less on their measure of productive activity than on the strength of their pressure on the power of the State. This latter power also had to look after the selling, as well as after the buying of raw materials. A well-disciplined and highly-intelligent working-class was necessary, a working-class which would recognise to what large extent the social prosperity, and therefore their own, depended on the productivity of their labour, in order, under these conditions, to make production successful and to keep it so. Moreover, from such a working class real production could be expected only if the necessary organising measures were taken which, apart from the workmen, as also apart from the State control and the consumers, would preserve the necessary influence on the single business concerns and the whole industrial branches; and also, if encouragement to work was created, which should supersede the dominating existence of capital.

From this time onwards, however, there was failing, not only organisation, but also the requisite intelligence and discipline of the working-classes. The more so, since the war and its results had put the most ignorant and most undeveloped sections of the proletariat in the wildest excitement. Certainly the Russian workman had derived a high sense of solidarity from his village commune; but the sphere of his influence was as limited as the village community itself, for it is really confined to a very small circle of his own personal comrades. The larger social unity is for him a matter of indifference. The unfortunate results arising from these circumstances the Bolshevists themselves regretted. Trotsky says in his book, " Work, Discipline and Order will save the Socialist Soviet Republic," page 17:

" The Revolution, which awakened a sense of human personality in the most oppressed and down-trodden, naturally took on at the beginning of its awakening an apparently anarchist character. This awakening of the elementary instincts of personality often shows a grossly egoistic or, to use a philosophical expression, an ego-centric character. It endeavours to acquire for itself all that it possibly can. It thinks only of itself, and is not at all inclined to have regard for the standpoint of the class in general. Hence the flood of all kinds of disorganising voices, and of individualistic, anarchistic, and grasping tendencies, which we observe especially in the broader spheres of the lower elements in the country, as well as in the midst of the earlier army, and also among certain elements of the working-classes."

These were quite other elements than those which appeared in the Paris Commune, where men contented themselves with a modest wage in order to further Socialism. Under such circumstances, the form taken by production in the expropriated concerns is clear. The wages were raised as high as was possible, and hence there was only an economy of labour. In order to facilitate this, work by agreement was abolished. Then there were occasions, such as in the case of the Poutilof works in Petersburg, which, in the period when they drew 96,000,000 roubles as a subsidy from the State, produced a total value of 50,000,000. It was only the unlimited employment of paper money that made it possible to avoid bankruptcy, which then seemed inevitable. If there was little work done in the factories, obviously the workmen withdrew, especially from the unpleasant, the dirty, and the heavy labour. How this kind of labour is to be established and assured in a Socialist community, in so far as it is indispensable, was a problem which has engaged the attention of Socialists of all times. Furier thought to solve it by engaging " gutter snipes " for dirty work, youths who in preference wallow in mud. But this humorous solution was clearly not satisfactory. The only solution, in fact, which is in accordance with Socialist principles, and which could promise any success, is that it demands of technical science the elimination of all injurious and disagreeable elements in work, which is by its nature wearisome and prejudicial to health. So long as this is not possible there remains no other course than to make this section of labour attractive by means of particular privileges, either extraordinarily high wages or extraordinarily short working hours.

The Bolsheviks discovered a new solution. It did not at all correspond with Socialist principles, but with the mass psychology of excited working masses. In other words, they introduced *compulsory labour*, not, however, compulsory labour for those who had hitherto been paid labourers. Why impose on them compulsory labour? Under the influence of new conditions one factory after the other, whether on account of lack of raw material or of transport difficulties, had to close down, so that the number of workers who could find no work increased. Oh, no! Compulsory labour was imposed only on those who had been deprived of all privileges under the excuse that they did not work, namely, the bourgeois. Instead of the universal formal democracy, the Soviet Republic established the proletarian democracy. Only those who worked should have political rights; only they should be sufficiently fed and protected by the State. The drones were to be deprived of all rights.

This was apparently a great Socialist idea, which had only one small error. For nearly two years already the Republic of the working men's councils had given the vote to the workers alone. And yet up to this very day no solution to the riddle " What constitutes a worker? " has been given. From different communists we get different answers. At the outset, these working men's councils were none other than representative bodies of the paid labourers of the large factories. As such, they formed definite though limited organisations, which were very important for the Revolution. The " council idea " then proceeded to substitute a Central Council of the working-men's councils for the National Assembly, which had arisen from the general elections. Nevertheless, the foundation of this Central Council would have been very shaky, if its establishment had been confined to the Working-men's Councils of the large factories. But as soon as they went outside this circle, and at the same time excluded the bourgeoisie from having a vote, they became utterly lost. The demarcation of the middle class from the working-class can never be accurately drawn. There will always be something arbitrary in such endeavour, which fact makes the council idea peculiarly liable to become a foundation for a purely dictatorial and arbitrary rule, but very little calculated to establish and build up a clear and systematic State constitution.

For instance, in the case of the educated class (intelligentsia) it rests entirely with the Soviet authorities whether they are to be reckoned as belonging to the middle class or not. The same applies to their right of voting, and also in respect to their being liable to compulsory labour.

In the Soviet Republic the bourgeois not only had to suffer the confiscation of all means of production and consumption, without any compensation whatever, and were not only deprived of all political rights;

they were, at the same time, the victims of oppression, and they alone were liable to compulsory labour! They are the only people in Russia who are compelled to work, and at the same time the very people who are deprived of the vote, because they do not work! Moreover, in Soviet Russia, a man is not put into the class of workers or bourgeoisie according to the occupation that he for the moment has, but according to the occupation that he had before the Revolution. The bourgeoisie in this respect appears in the Soviet Republic as a special human species, whose characteristics are ineradicable.   Just as a nigger remains a nigger, a Mongolian a Mongolian, whatever his appearance and however he may dress; so a bourgeois remains a bourgeois, even if he becomes a beggar, or lives by his work.   And how he lives indeed!

The bourgeoisie are compelled to work, but they have not the right to choose the work that they understand, and which best corresponds to their abilities.   On the contrary, they are forced to carry on the most filthy and most objectionable kind of labour.   In return they receive not increased rations, but the very lowest, which scarce suffice to appease their hunger.   Their food rations equal only a quarter of those of the soldiers, and of the working-men who are employed in the factories run by the Soviet Republic.   Where these latter receive one pound of bread, the former get only a quarter of a pound; and where again the latter get sixteen pounds of potatoes, the others have only four.   From all this we perceive not a sign of any attempt to place the proletariat on a higher level, to work out a " new and higher form of life," but merely the thirst for vengeance on the part of the proletariat in its most primitive form. It thinks to gain happiness by being able to trample down those men who, by their destiny, have been in more favourable circumstances, who are better clothed, better housed and better educated than they themselves.

In setting free this " will " as the motive force of the Revolution, the Bolshevists have let things go much further, in certain cases, than even they themselves have wished.   Thus, for instance, the idea that the bourgeois of bygone days have now become merely beasts of burden, deprived of all rights, caused the workers who formerly were in the employ of such bourgeoisie to issue the following manifesto of the Working Men's Councils of Murzilovka:

" The Soviet gives herewith full power to Comrade Gregory Sareieff, according to his choice and orders, and for use in the artillery division, which is quartered in Murzilovka, in the district of Briantz, to *requisition sixty women and girls* of the bourgeois and financier class, and to hand them over to the barracks."   16th September, 1918 (published by Dr. Nath Wintsch-Malejeff, " What are the Bolsheviks Doing?" Lausanne, 1919, page 10).

We should be doing an injustice to place the responsibility for this manifesto on the Bolsheviks, for it was certainly just as contrary to their wishes, as were the September massacres to the men of the Convention. But the thought that, in one single local Soviet organisation, hatred and contempt towards the bourgeois could reach such a stage is horrible in the extreme; for these men are deprived not only of all political rights, but even of the most elementary considerations of human dignity.

THE GROWTH OF THE PROLETARIAT.

It is only natural that not even the Bolsheviks could entirely yield to a mass psychology that took on such forms. After they had expropriated the bourgeois class, and declared them "free as the air," and had made the proletariat into a "sacred entity," they attempted to inculcate some necessary improvements in this "sacred entity," which really should have been the pre-conditions of all socialisation and expropriation.

"We have known for some time past," said Trotsky, "that we lack the necessary organisation, the necessary discipline, and the necessary historical education. We knew all this, but it did not prevent us in any way from endeavouring, with open eyes, to acquire power for ourselves. We were convinced that we could in time learn and arrange everything." ("Work, Discipline, etc.," page 16.)

But would Trotsky undertake to get on a locomotive and set it going, in the conviction that he would, during the journey, "learn and arrange everything"? There is no doubt that he would be quite capable of doing this, but would he have the necessary time? Would not the train be very likely soon to become derailed or explode? One must have acquired something of the qualities necessary to drive an engine, before one attempts to set it going. In like manner the proletariat should have acquired those qualities, which are indispensable for organisation and production, if it wishes to undertake this task. For such organisation endures no vacuum, no condition of void, no standing still; and least of all a condition such as that created by the war, which has deprived us of all means of equipment, so that we have to live from hand to mouth, and are threatened with death from starvation, as a result of the cessation of production. Lenin himself already regards it as necessary to put a check on the process of expropriation.

"If we should now endeavour to continue any further expropriation of capital at the rate we did formerly, we should certainly suffer defeat. It is perfectly clear and obvious to every thinking man, that the task of organising the proletarian finance has remained subordinate to our work of the immediate expropriation of the expropriators." ("The Immediate Duties of the Soviet Power," page 14.)

But Lenin is in no spirit of renunciation. On the contrary, he still declares that, despite all, the Soviets would win in "the campaign against capital"; for the process of the development of the Russian proletariat is proceeding in giant strides. He says:

"As a condition of the increase of the productivity of labour, there appears an increase in the culture and education of the masses of the population. This increase is proceeding at a remarkable rate, thanks to the 'impetus' to life and initiative, which has begun to show itself deep in the souls of the people." (page 33.)

The rise in higher education of the masses of the people can take a double form. It may proceed in an orderly and systematic way through the schools. In this respect there is an enormous amount still to accomplish in Russia. An adequate system of popular education demands enormous means and a flourishing state of production, which provides a great surplus for such services. But the state of production in Russia brings such wretched results that the school system has had to suffer most grievously. Certainly the Bolsheviks have been striving all they can to spread knowledge of art and science among the masses; but all their endeavours have been frightfully hampered by the changed economic conditions in which they find themselves. From this it is clear that a speedy rise in education, which would make possible a rapid and satisfactory increase in production, cannot be expected. On the contrary, this increase in production is a pre-condition of the rise in education. Grown men, however, for the most part, do not learn any more in the schools that the State or the community sets up, but much more in the school of life.

The best means of education are provided for them in a democracy, in which absolute freedom of discussion and publicity are essential. But this imposes on every party the obligation to strive for the emancipation of the souls of the people; and to put every member of the community in a position to examine the arguments of all sides, so that, by such means, each may arrive at some independent judgment.

Finally, class struggle takes over from democracy its best features; for in democracy each party addresses itself to the whole social community. Each party certainly defends definite class interests; but it is compelled to show every side of these interests, which are intimately connected with the general interest of the whole social community. In this way modern State democracy is superior to the narrowness of village church policy, as also to the cliquish nature of professional politics. In democracy the horizon of the masses becomes enormously extended by participation in politics. All these possibilities of education of the people become simply shattered if, as the Soviet Republic has done, democracy is set aside in favour of an autocracy of the working-men's council, which deprives every " bourgeois " of his rights, and abolishes the freedom of the press. The particular interests of the wage-earners in this way become detached from general social interests, and the working man himself is, at the same time, denied an independent examination of the arguments that arise in the struggle of the various classes and parties. For this examination is already settled for him by a patronising authority, which anxiously tries to keep from him every thought and every feeling, which might cause doubts to arise in his heart as to the divine nature of the Soviet system. Naturally enough, this is exactly what should happen in the interests of truth. The poor ignorant people should be prevented from being deceived and poisoned by a bourgeois Press, with all its enormous and powerful machinery.   But where in present-day Russia is this powerful machinery to be found, which grants to the bourgeois newspapers a superiority over the Bolshevik papers?   Apart from all this, the bitterness of the Bolshevik enslaving of the press is employed not merely against the bourgeois papers alone, but against the whole of the press that does not swear allegiance to the existing system of government.

The justification of this system simply proceeds on the naïve assumption that there really exists an absolute truth, and that the Communists alone are in possession of that truth.   It also proceeds on another assumption, namely, that all journalists are, by their very nature, liars; whereas only the Communists are the fanatics of truth. Everywhere there are to be found liars as well as fanatics, who accept as true everything that they see.   But the lie flourishes best in those places where it has no control to fear, and where, moreover, the press of a certain tendency alone has the right to speak.   In this way it simply has *carte blanche* to lie, and this encourages those elements that tend to deception.   Therefore it is turned to account the more desperate the position of those in power, and the more they fear the truth.   The truth in regard to information is in no way strengthened by the abolition of the freedom of the press.   On the contrary, it is most adversely affected thereby.   As to the truth of conceptions and ideas, we must say with Pilate: " What is truth ? " There is no such thing as absolute truth.   There is merely a process of knowledge, and this process is in every way impaired, and with it also men's possibilities of acquiring knowledge, if one party uses its power to monopolise its own conceptions as the one blessed truth, and seeks to suppress every other opinion. It is not to be doubted that the idealists among the Bolsheviks have acted in perfect good faith, in believing that they were in complete possession of the truth, and that only sheer perverseness could make others think differently from them. But we must equally attribute good faith to the men of the Holy Inquisition of Spain. The rise in culture and education among the masses of the people certainly received and impetus under its regime.

There is certainly a difference between the Inquisitors and the leaders of the Soviet Republic. The former did not in any way desire the material and spiritual improvement of the masses on this earthly sphere. They wished merely to ensure their souls for the future life. The Soviet people believed they could, by means of the methods of the Inquisition, raise the masses of the people in every way. They do not at all see how very much they are degrading them. Besides, a high standard of popular education, a high " morale " among the masses is a pre-condition of Socialism, a morale which shows itself not merely in strong social instincts and feelings of solidarity, of sympathy and of self-sacrifice, but also in the extension of these feelings beyond the narrow circles of one's comrades to the generality of mankind. We found such a morale strongly developed among the proletarians of the Paris Commune. It is utterly failing in the masses of the people who mostly constitute the Bolshevik proletariat.

But this " morale " must be created at all costs, so says Trotsky. " This communist morale, my comrades, we are in duty bound to preach, to support, to develop and to establish. That is the finest and highest task of our party, in all departments of its activity." ("Work, Discipline," etc., page 21).

Yes, but does Trotsky really believe that you can create morale overnight? That can develop but slowly. On the other hand, the encouragement to production suffers no delay. If the morale of the communists has not formed itself before the beginning of socialisation, it will be too late to develop it after expropriation has taken place. And how is it to be developed? It shall be preached. As if ever in this world anything had come from moral sermons. Whenever Marxists base their hopes on moral sermons, they merely show into how deep a blind alley they have fallen. But indeed this new morale is not to be merely preached, but supported. But again, how? " Morale " is the product of our lives and activities. From these it derives its nourishment and its form. The higher morale which the struggling proletariat develops depends on two factors. Being the poorest and weakest members of society, the proletariat can only assert itself by the most intimate co-operation. Sympathy and self-sacrifice of the individual are regarded in its ranks as the highest quality, in opposition to the capitalist class, in which the individual makes his wealth at the expense of the masses, without any consideration as to how he gains it. But even the strong feelings of solidarity can have a directly anti-social effect, if they are confined to a narrow circle, which seeks to gain its advantage at the cost of the rest of society, like the nobility, or the bureaucracy, or an officers' corps. What, however, does raise the solidarity of the modern proletariat to the height of social morale is its extension to the whole of humanity. The extension of such solidarity springs from the consciousness that the proletariat cannot emancipate itself without emancipating the whole of the human race. Long ago the youthful Engels hoped to derive from a knowledge of this fact the greatest aids to an improvement of the proletarian morale. He declares in his " Position of the Working Classes in England," (2nd edition, page 299) :—

" In proportion as the proletariat assimilates socialist and communist elements, the revolution abates in bloodshed and rage. In its very principles Communism stands over and above the division of the bourgeois and the proletariat. It recognises this division in its historical significance for the present day, but does not regard it as justified for the future. Communism wishes to remove this division. So long as this division is maintained, it recognises the bitterness of the proletarian against his oppressor as a necessary evil, as the most forceful lever to be employed in the labour agitation that is just taking place; but it seeks to rise above this bitterness, because it represents the cause of humanity, and not merely the cause of the working-class alone. Nevertheless, no communist ever wishes to wreak vengeance on the individual, nor does he really believe that the individual bourgeois can act differently in the existing circumstances than he actually does. The more, therefore, the English working man adopts Socialist ideas, the more will his present bitterness, which if it remains as it does can achieve nothing, become superfluous; and the more will all action against the bourgeois lose in brutality and cruelty. If it were in any way possible to make the whole proletariat communist before the struggle began, the struggle itself would proceed on most peaceful lines. But that is no longer possible. It is already too late. (Engels expected in 1845, the imminent outbreak of the Revolution which, however, came in 1848, but on the Continent and not in England, and the Revolution itself was not proletarian.—Editor.) I believe meanwhile that until the outbreak of the quite open and direct war of the poor against the rich, which has become inevitable in England, takes place, at least sufficient clearness over the social question will have spread among the proletariat; and that, with the help of coming events, the communist party will be in a position to overcome in time the brutal elements of the Revolution, and to yield to a Ninth Thermidor.''

(9th Thermidor was the day on which Robespierre was overthrown, and the Paris Regiment of Terror collapsed.) Such a similar collapse Engels wished to prevent; and for this purpose he urged that all the communists should set to work, by eliminating from the proletarian class-struggle its coarseness and brutality against the bourgeois, and by placing in the forefront the general interests of humanity. It is obvious that Engels understood communism in an utterly different sense from the Bolsheviks of the present day. What Engels wanted, those Russian Socialists who are in opposition to the Bolsheviks are now fighting for. Bolshevism triumphed over its social opponents, by making the ferocity and brutality of the coming labour agitation "the motive force of the Revolution." This Bolshevism did, by degrading the social movement, by turning the cause of humanity into a mere cause of the working-men, and by announcing that to the wage earners alone belonged power (alongside of the poorest peasants in the country); further, by condemning all men to be deprived of their rights, if they did not blow the same trumpet as they did, and reducing them to the deepest misery; and further, by abolishing the different classes and virtually creating a new class of helots out of the existing bourgeois. Hence, by transforming what should have been the social struggle for liberty, and for the raising of the whole of humanity on a higher plane, into an outbreak of bitterness and revenge, which led to the worst abuses and tortures, Bolshevism has demoralised the proletariat, instead of raising it to a higher level of morale. It has further increased the demoralisation, by separating the " expropriating of the expropriators " from the intimate connection with the creation of a new social organisation, with which alone it can form a social element. This procedure soon extended in application from the means of production to the means of consumption. From this it was an easy step to brigandage, such as has been idealised in Stenka Razin.

"The masses had without any difficulty understood the negative programme of Bolshevism, which was that one need not fight. It did not recognise any more obligations. One had only to take, to seize, and to appropriate what one could get; or as Lenin so wonderfully puts it, one should steal what has been stolen." (D. Gavronski, "The Balance of Russian Bolshevism," Berlin, 1919, page 39.)

It is in keeping with this conception that the robber captain has already received his memorial in the Soviet Republic. In this manner Bolshevism "supported" and preached the new communist morale, without which socialistic construction is impossible. It meant nothing other than the increasing demoralisation of further sections of the Russian proletariat. This was a feature over which the idealists among the Bolsheviks themselves were horrified; but they could only see the appearance without recognising its cause, for that would have meant upsetting their whole system of government. In desperation they looked round for a means that should give the communist morale to the masses. They could discover nothing, these Marxists, these bold revolutionaries and innovators, except the miserable expedient with which the old society endeavoured to absolve itself from the results of its own sins, namely, the *tribunal, prison and execution,* in other words, Terrorism. Lenin writes in his book (already several times quoted) on the "Immediate work of the Soviet Republic" (page 47):

"The tribunal is the instrument in education to discipline. There is not enough recognition of the very simple and obvious fact that, if all the misery that has befallen Russia, hunger, and unemployment have made their appearance, this misfortune cannot be overcome by mere force and energy, but by a general all-embracing organisation and discipline; that everyone, therefore, is responsible for misery, hunger, and unemployment who overrides the discipline determined by labour in any particular business concerned, or in any particular affair; and that it is one's duty to

find the culprits, bring them before the tribunal, and
punish them mercilessly."

Thus, with merciless punishment, the Russian
proletariat is to have pummelled into it the communist
morale it lacks, in order to make it ripe for Socialism.
But never was morale raised by merciless punishment.
On the contrary, all that remained of it has always
gone under.   Merciless punishment was a necessary
evil of the old order of things, when people did not
know how to act differently, since the way towards a
better morale and a better condition of life was barred
to them. A Socialist regime, which could find no other
way to awaken the proletariat to a higher morale than
by means of merciless court proceedings proves its own
state of bankruptcy.

THE DICTATORSHIP.

It seems as if Lenin himself does not expect any
particular incentive to morale from his own tribunals;
for immediately after his demand for such tribunals
he makes another claim for " dictatorial and unlimited
powers for the individual leaders of all concerns "
(page 49).   " Every great industry, which represents
the origin and foundation of Socialism, demands the
unconditional and the strictest unity of purpose. How
can the strictest unity of will and purpose be assured?
By the subordination of the will of thousands to the
will of an individual.   This subordination, which
embodies an ideal understanding and sense of
discipline on the part of those occupied in combined
labour, bears some resemblance to the subtle direction
of an orchestra conductor.   It can claim dictatorial
powers in their severest form, if no ideal sense of
discipline and understanding exists " (page 51).

Hitherto we have always assumed that understanding and discipline on the part of the working-classes

were to be the necessary conditions for the development and growth of the proletariat, without which real
Socialism could not be possible. Lenin himself says
at the beginning of this book from which we have just
quoted :
    " Such revolution can only be realised with success,
if it has the co-operation of the majority of the population, especially of the majority of the working-
classes." After he has shown that Socialism cannot
be the work of a minority, nor even of the majority of
the population, but only " especially " and not
exclusively of the working-classes; and after he has,
by these admissions, justified democracy against his
own will, he continues :—" Only when the proletariat
and the poorest sections of the peasantry have acquired
for themselves sufficient self-consciousness, strength of
ideas, self-sacrifice and determination, can the triumph
of the Socialist Revolution be assured." Nevertheless, its triumph is to be assured, it would seem,
through the dictatorship of the tribunals and of the
heads of factories.
    " The Revolution has just destroyed the oldest, the
strongest, and the heaviest chains, by which the
masses were held in bondage under threat of the knout.
Such was true of yesterday. To-day, however, this
same revolution indeed in the interests of Socialism
(page 52), demands the absolute subordination of the
masses to the single will of the leaders of labour."
    The freedom which they gained yesterday for them-
selves is to-day to be taken from them, since the
masses apparently have not acquired sufficient " self-
consciousness, strength of ideas, self-sacrifice and
determination." But on page 7 the impracticability
of Socialism as the result of the lack of these qualities
has been shown, whereas on page 52, in the interests
of Socialism, " the absolute subordination " of the
immature masses to dictatorial leaders is demanded.
By this means their position will sink below the level

of that which they had on the old capitalist system. For in that system they were subordinated to capital, but, nevertheless, not absolutely subordinate. Lenin certainly comforts himself and the public by asserting that, in distinction from the old capitalist system of management, this dictatorship will become possible as the result of the co-operation of the masses of the workers, and of those who were formerly exploited; and, further, through the organisations, which will be so constructed that through them the masses will be roused, and will, by their active efforts, ultimately achieve something of historical importance. The Soviet organisations belong to this kind of organisation (page 51). In what way the exclusion and suppression of any kind of criticism is to help forward the awakening of the masses and their encouragement to creative activity has already been shown. The Soviet organisation alters nothing in this respect. How can this iron form of dictatorship of individuals, " with the absolute subordination of the masses," be realised through the organisation of the masses into individual activity? Whoever is to be elected by the masses or deposed by them, or whoever is to be re-elected will always remain dependent on them, for he cannot carry anything through which does not meet with their approval. He can certainly attempt to break the obstinacy of individual members of the organisation which elects him, if they should be in opposition to the majority; but he would very soon be at the end of his tether if he should wish to impose on the majority, against their will, his own ideas and orders. For this reason a personal dictatorship and democracy are incompatible. Such is also true for the Soviet democracy. Lenin does indeed declare that these remarks are liable to criticism, but vehemence is substituted for strength in his arguments, for he can give no other answer than : —

" If we are not anarchists we accept the fact that the State as such is necessary, that is, we accept the need for *compulsion* in the period of transition from Capitalism to Socialism " (page 50).

With this we are in complete agreement. Even democracy itself does not exclude a certain kind of compulsion; but the only kind of compulsion it concedes is that of the majority over the minority. The compulsion necessary for the transition from Capitalism to Socialism is the compulsion of the majority of the workers over the minority of the capitalists; but this is not the case in the second stage of the Revolution, of which Lenin himself speaks, and in which the proletariat has already broken its chains. Here it is a question of the compulsion exercised by single individuals over the masses of the workers. That this form of compulsion is incompatible with democracy Lenin does not attempt to show. He seeks rather to make it compatible, by a sort of conjuror's trick, by attempting to show that, since compulsion must be exercised by the great masses upon individual capitalists in order to bring about Socialism, and since such Socialism is perfectly well compatible with democracy, every form of compulsion which might be applied with a view to introducing Socialism is compatible with democracy, even if it should represent the absolute power of single individuals over the masses. He says :—

" Hence there is no fundamental opposition between the Soviet (i.e., Socialist) democracy and the delegation of the dictatorial powers to certain individuals."

That may be; but it would only show that the Soviet democracy is a very peculiar structure, which one could employ to uphold any form of arbitary domination, provided one merely gave it the name of Socialism. If an absolute subordination of the workers in a business concern to their chief is to be brought about, he ought not to be elected by them, but should be put in command by some power superior to them. In such a case the business council in the concern should have nothing to say. Moreover, the Central Executive Committee, which appoints these dictators, would itself have acquired dictatorial power; and so the Soviets would be reduced to mere shadows, and the masses represented by them would lose all real power. A working-class which lacked " self-consciousness, strength of ideas, self-sacrifice and determination " is incapable itself of choosing its own dictator, through whom it is to be raised to a higher level, and to whom it must bend its will, if he should demand of them deeds which required " self-consciousness, strength of ideas, self-sacrifice and determination." It is as far from doing this as was Münchausen of extricating himself from the bog by means of his own hair. And where are these dictators with the necessary moral force, as well as the intellectual qualities and superiority, to be found? Every form of arbitrary rule carries with it the seed of corruption of the authority itself, be this a single individual or a small coterie. Only exceptional characters can remain exempt from pernicious consequences. Are we to assume that the Russian dictators are through and through all characters like this? Lenin promises that they are to be very carefully sifted.

" We wish to pursue our path by seeking, with all caution and patience, to examine the right organisations, and to take account of the men with clear intelligence and practical sense—men who combine enthusiasm for Socialism with the gift of being able, without undue bluster (and uninfluenced by the noise and bewilderment) to hold together a large number of men, and make them combine in determined, unified, and concerted labour within the framework of the Soviet organisations. Only such men, after the tenfold examination through which they go by passing from the most simple to the most difficult tasks, are to be placed in responsible positions as heads of administration. *We have not yet learned to do this. We shall learn*" (pages 41 and 42).

He does not say who is to be understood under this " we." Obviously not the ignorant, undisciplined, bewildered masses; more likely the higher authority, the Central Executive Committee. But even this body has not yet learnt the art of selecting aright leaders of massed labour. It promises to learn this difficult art. No time limit is given. Only this is certain, that at the present moment the selection of these leaders is proceeding in a highly unsatisfactory manner. The necessary capacity of the men at the head is lacking, just as much as the necessary maturity of the masses.

After they have been expropriating and are now proceeding to organisation, they find that they have first to set about learning—even learning how to choose aright the higher administrators of State economy.

CORRUPTION.

And what elements are insinuating themselves into the new regime! " No single profound and powerful mass movement has ever taken place in history without dubious means, without adventurers and swindlers who bleed inexperienced novices, without boasters and mob orators, without senseless vacillation and stupidity, without needless fuss, without attempts on the part of the individual leaders to attempt twenty different things without pursuing one to its end " (Lenin, " The immediate work, etc.," page 40).

There is no doubt that every great mass movement has to suffer from such pernicious influences. We in Germany have also been made to feel this; but the Russian Soviet regime has given proof besides of

certain characteristics peculiar to it.   In the first
place, the novices were never so " inexperienced " as
they are in Russia.   That was inevitable.   Under the
absolutist regime all the elements who were striving
upwards were denied all chance of insight, and still
more all chance of participation in the administration
of the State and of the community, as well as in all
forms   of   higher   organisation   and   administrative
activity.

The interest of the revolutionaries, particularly of
the most impatient and most violent elements among
them, was concentrated on the struggle against the
police and secret conspiracy.   One has no right to
reproach them for their inexperience, when they suddenly came to power.   But this inexperience represents an important feature, which proves how unripe
Russia was for Socialism at the time of the outbreak of
the Revolution.   Socialism can still less be carried out
by ignorant and undisciplined masses, the more
inexperienced the novices are who have to show the
way.   It is a further proof that the schooling and
education of the masses, as well as of their leaders, in
democracy is a necessary condition of Socialism.   It
is impossible in one bound to leap from Absolutism into
a Socialist society.   Again, the difference between the
Soviet regime and the earlier great massed movements
is shown in the fact that the Soviet has abolished the
best   means   for   exposing   the   adventurers,   the
swindlers, the boasters and the brawlers, namely, the
freedom of the Press.   These undesirable elements
were thus exempt from all criticism by people who had
expert knowledge.   They had to do only with ignorant
workmen and soldiers, as well as with inexperienced
innovators, and they flourished exceedingly.   Certainly
the leaders of the Bolsheviks have undertaken to learn
how to separate the wheat from the chaff, and to distinguish the true Socialists from the swindlers and the
rogues.   But long before this has been " learnt " pro-

duction has failed, as the result of the backward state
of the Russian working-classes, and even threatens to
come to a complete standstill. Their only hope of
arresting this catastrophe lies in a dictatorship of the
leaders, but they must give these leaders dictatorship,
without being in the position to make adequate choice.
Hence this kind of dictatorship, which from the outset is
open to much criticism, can only work to disadvantage.
Just as they first of all indulged in expropriation, and
only then began to organise; so now they appoint
dictators, and only afterwards attempt to learn the
method of choosing them rightly.   Such absurdities
were inevitable as soon as they began to introduce
Socialism arbitrarily, and without any relation to
actual conditions. But the Soviet regime is not only
endangered through the incursion of " adventurers and
swindlers," whom it cannot judge and examine
accurately. It suffers from a danger, which is no less
serious, from the fact that it alienates those members
who have the highest character and who, intellectually,
are among the most prominent.   Without the collaboration of the educated and intellectual elements,
Socialism at the present stage of production is
impossible. So long as Socialism was in the stage of
propaganda, so long as it was merely a question of
bringing the proletariat to a consciousness of its place
in society and of its tasks and obligations for the
future arising therefrom, Socialism had need of
the educated elements—whether these were men of
universal education, drawn from among the middle
classes, or self-educated men, who had sprung from
the proletariat. But it needed them only for the carrying out and popularising of its theories. Here it was
not a question of quantity, but solely of quality.

But it is quite different at the present time, when
we are in the period in which Socialism in a practical
form is to be introduced. Just as a capitalist system
of production and the capitalist state could not exist

without the help of numerous reliable and scientific men, social production and the State system, which is dominated by the working classes, requires such help equally urgently. Without such assistance, or in opposition to it, no Socialism is possible. For practical participation in the establishment of Socialism, as well as in the development and propagation of Socialist theories, a passionate devotion to the great cause of the emancipation of the human race is not essential. What is most necessary is, that a large section of them at least should be convinced of the possibility and advantage of Socialist production, so that no sacrifice of intelligence is necessary if one wishes to co-operate. If in the matter of manual labour an improved production is impossible with any kind of compulsory labour, this is all the more the case in the sphere of intellectual work.

The removal of doubt on the part of the educated as to the practical introduction of Socialism, and the willingness of such elements to co-operate in its construction and development, as soon as the necessary power arises, belong to the necessary conditions of Socialist production, to the conditions to which society will have progressed, if it is to be ripe for Socialism. The importance of these conditions will be all the more obvious the more other necessary conditions of Socialism are to hand; so that a recognition of the practicability of Socialism will lead the unbiassed educated classes to a conviction of its sound reasonableness.

This importance of the educated classes the Bolsheviks did not recognise at first. For since at the beginning they merely served to increase the blind passion of the soldiers, the peasants and the town labourers, the masses of the educated were from the very beginning hostile to the Bolsheviks, and even the Socialists among them; because they recognised that Russia was not yet ripe for the kind of immediate socialisation which the Bolsheviks had undertaken.

They did not trouble to think about the treatment which was meted out to the " intelligentsia." A man of this class, for instance, would be expelled from the factory which the workers alone wished to manage. He was deprived of all political rights, since the authority of the Workmen's Council granted to manual labourers alone the right to vote. He was expropriated, so far as he had any possessions, and was deprived of every means of living his refined form of life. He was even condemned later on to compulsory labour and to death by starvation.

The Bolsheviks thought at first to get along without the " intelligentsia," without the experts. Tsarism was of the opinion that a general was capable of filling any and every position in the State without any special qualification or education. The Soviet Republic took over from Tsarism, along with many other ideas, this one also; only in the place of the general they put the proletariat. The theoreticians among the Bolsheviks called this procedure " the development of Socialism from science to action." One could better describe it as " the development of Socialism from science to dilettantism."

As is generally the case with the Soviet Republic, it allows itself to be guided by mere instinct, and not by real insight into the actual circumstances. Thus it happened that they discovered, after the child had fallen into the well, what was necessary, and so they tried to cover up the well. They sought to attract the educated to work apart from any compulsory labour, as had been the case some time before, and, indeed, to do work for which they were suited, and which they understood. Whereupon the educated classes who entered the service of the Government ceased to count as bourgeois, to be treated and ill-treated as such. They rose in the circle of the " active and working " population by performing " productive " and " useful " labour. They were protected from

expropriation and received adequate salary.   Since it
was not conviction, but only fear of ill-treatment
that drove most of these educated into the service
of the Government, naturally enough their work was
in reality neither very productive nor very useful.
Trotsky complains about this, for instance, in his essay
on " Work, Discipline, etc.," quoted above; he says :—
    " The first epoch of the fight against the sabotage
(of the intellectuals) consisted in mercilessly destroying
the organisations of the saboteurs.   That was
necessary, and therefore right.   Now in the period
where the power of the Soviets has become assured,
this struggle against the saboteurs must take the form
of transforming the saboteurs of yesterday into
servants, into administrators, and technical managers,
wherever the new regime demands it."
    Trotsky, therefore, implies that the " necessary and
therefore right " way to make these intellectuals
servants and leaders of socialisation is, first of all,
mercilessly to trample them under foot.   The result of
this he himself gives us :—
    " We have destroyed the old forms of sabotage,
and swept away the old officials with an iron broom.
The substitutes for these old officials proved themselves
to be by no means first-class material in any branch
whatsoever of administration.   On the one hand, the
posts that have become vacant were filled by comrades of each party, who had done all the " spade
work," and who had been schooled in the revolution.
They formed the best elements, the fighters, the
honourable men, the men who were not self-seekers.
On the other hand, there appeared on the scene
fortune-seekers, social failures who under the old
regime had been, so to speak, without occupation.
When, therefore, it was necessary to get tens of
thousands of new qualified labour at one stroke, it is
not to be wondered at if many intruders succeeded in
penetrating into the new regime.   We must also

admit that many of the Socialist comrades, who are now at work in different offices and institutions, have by no means shown themselves to be always capable of organising creative and energetic labour. We can follow the movements of such comrades in the minis-terial offices, especially of those in the ranks of the October Bolsheviks, who work four or five hours a day, and not very intensively at that; whereas our whole position now demands the most strenuous labour, not out of fear, but from a sense of duty.''

That was the necessary, though by no means the right consequence of a policy which sought to win the educated classes, not through conviction, but merely through kicks from behind as well as from the front.

Another means was devised to increase the supply of active labour. The Paris Commune of 1871 reduced the pay of State officials, and decided on the sum of 6,000 francs as a maximum salary. The Soviet Republic endeavoured to do likewise; but this would not work, so they had to revert to the old system. Lenin remarks in this connection :—

''We must needs return to the old bourgeois methods, and establish very high payment for all 'service rendered' by the best of the bourgeois experts. It is clear that such a measure is a com-promise, and somewhat of a departure from the principles of the Paris Commune and of every prole-tarian power. . . . It is clear that such a measure means not only the standstill—in certain departments and to a certain degree—of the offensive against capital, but also a retrograde step in our socialising power as a Soviet.'' (''The Immediate Work of the Soviet Power,'' page 19.)

But Lenin implies that it cannot be otherwise, and he is perfectly right. The necessity for high salaries can arise from two causes. The bigger the concern, the greater the number of its workers. So much more important under equal circumstances, therefore, is the

H

mass of the gross value which it delivers. If the workman produces value equivalent to five shillings a day,
the concern with a hundred workmen will produce to
the value of 500 shillings a day, and one with a
thousand workmen will produce 5,000 shillings a day.
The bigger the concern, the more difficult it is to
organise and guide it, and all the rarer is the necessary
efficiency for its organisation.   But all the greater
will be the means which the owner or owners of the
concern will have at their disposal, in order to engage
the services of such select equipment. In proportion,
therefore, as these large industries increase, the
salaries of their heads increase also, and finally reach
vast dimensions.   With this circumstance the State
administration has to reckon. If it does not raise pro-
portionately the salaries of its higher officials, it
must be prepared to find that private industry will
attract them away—so far as they are at all capable,
and not mere holders of sinecures. In this way the
State administration becomes impoverished, and that
is one of the reasons why State economy is unable to
cope with competition of private enterprise.

It is questionable whether the Commune, once it had
become established, and whether industry on a large
scale, once it had been developed on capitalistic lines
under the Commune, instead of becoming socialised,
which was possible, could have maintained this system
of fixed salaries at 6,000 frs. The decree issued on April
2nd shows the small bourgeois character of the Paris
industry at that time. Moreover it proves the disin-
terestedness of the members of the Commune.   We
have already referred to the well-known example of
the Financial Minister, Jourde.   Competition, however, arising from a flourishing and powerful private
industry in Soviet Russia makes it impossible to force
up the wages of the most skilled " specialists "; for
either such an industry is expropriated and ruined, or it
soon deprives the private owner of all value.   High

wages can have only one object. They are calculated to overcome the objection to serve the Soviet Republic, which objection the most capable among the educated secretly cherish in their hearts, and also to awaken their interest for the new regime.

Since the way of conviction does not work, and since the lash of hunger does not obtain any startling results, there remains but one way open to buy the people, and that is, to provide for them at least such conditions as they had under the capitalist system. We now see what are the elements which are to become leaders of Socialist production in the Soviet Republic. On the one side a few old conspirators, honourable fighters of blameless intentions, yet in matters of business merely inexperienced novices; and on the other side, numerous educated men who, against their own convictions, either as mere seekers try to adapt themselves to the new power, as they would adapt themselves to any other power, if occasion arose; or who are driven through fear and hunger and punishment; or, finally, such men as allowed themselves to be bought by high wages. They are, as Trotsky admits, by no means first-class elements. Moreover, in so far as they know anything at all, they do not belong to the best, the worthiest of their kind. People among them, who at the same time possessed strong character as well as business knowledge, were as rare as white crows. In the hands of such elements dictatorial power has now been placed in order to save Socialism; a power which the workers have to accept without opposition. Such power tends to corrupt even the best. In this respect it is often entrusted to people who are corrupt from the very start.

In the midst of the general misery and the general expropriation they gather together in their hands the beginnings of a new capitalism. Of course the production of commodities proceeds, and must proceed; since agricultural activity, regarded as private enterprise, as a matter of fact represents the production of commodities, and influences life as a whole. For this reason the peasant community has less and less of surplus stocks to sell. The Soviet Republic grants full power in a village to the poor peasants, who possess so little land that they can produce no surplus in foodstuffs. From the well-to-do peasants all surplus commodities are to be taken without any compensation, and placed at the service of the State granaries. This practice, in so far as it is ever carried out, can take place only once, for, in the following year, the well-to-do peasant will take very good care that he does not produce more than he himself needs. In this way the returns of agirculture will be limited. Whatever of surplus stock the peasant produces, in spite of this, he conceals, and merely sells it secretly to the profiteers.

At the same time industry comes to a standstill. As a consequence, the State expenditure can only be covered by a new paper money. Hence, as at the time of the French Revolution, and as again at the present day, although in a less degree in Germany, there flourish speculators, profiteers, and smugglers. Formerly they were guillotined. Nowadays it is the fashion to shoot them. But the failure is the same. The only result is that, at the present day, just as much as in 1793, the uncertain nature of the capital thus acquired by swindlers increases, as well as the amount of the bribes that the new dictators demand, and which they get if, by chance, an incautious person should fall into their net. Even that in its turn becomes a fresh basis for the collecting together of new property.

Whoever is anxious for further information over this bribery system of the new Russian bureaucracy should turn to Gavronsky's " Balance of the Russian Revolution," which, from page 58 and several pages onwards, is full of accounts of bribery and corruption.

How shall one get the better of these new " dictators," before whom the working masses are to bow
without opposition? As in its attempts to " moralise "
the masses, the Soviet Government knows no better
means of " moralising " its leaders than by the threat
of tribunals. If the dictatorship of the proletariat
is to be over-ridden by the dictatorship of its organisers,
these in their turn will be over-ruled by the dictatorship of the tribunals.

A network of revolutionary tribunals and extraordinary commissions has been formed " to oppose the
counter-revolution, speculation, and abuse." They have
the arbitrary power to condemn anyone who shall be
denounced to them, and at their discrimination to
shoot those of whom they do not approve; that is to
say, all those speculators and profiteers whom they
catch, as well as their accomplices among the Soviet
officials. They do not stop merely at that, but
involve every honourable man who dares to criticise
their fearful misrule. Under the collective name of
" counter-revolution " every form of opposition is
included, in whatever circles it arises and from whatever motives it springs, whatever the means employed
and whatever the ends aimed for. But unfortunately
this summary procedure has no result.

As often as not the sincere fighters among the
Bolsheviks become indignant, when they realise that
these extraordinary commissions, which are the last
hope for the cleansing of the Revolution, are themselves likewise corrupt. Gawronsky quotes (page 61)
the following heart-cry of the weekly journal of the
special commission : —

" From all sides there reach us news that not
only worthless elements, but direct criminals, are
endeavouring to slip into the commissions, and
especially into commissions in the various local
districts." Gawronsky also mentions people (page 62)
who have shown that this attempt at intrusion is not

only made, but very often made with success. So runs an article out of " The Will to Labour," the central organ of Revolutionary Communism, October 10th, 1918.

" Fresh in our memory there are still cases in which the local Soviets have been literally terrorised by the special and extraordinary Soviets. Naturally a local selection was made. In the Soviets the better elements remained, whereas in the extraordinary com- missions were to be found bands of men who were ready for any kind of brigandage. Hence there is nothing left of the programme for the renovation of humanity by means of Socialism on Bolshevik methods, except two or three sincere strugglers in the midst of an ever growing morass of ignorance, corruption, and desperation, which extends further and further, and finally threatens to engulf and drown them."

THE CHANGE IN BOLSHEVISM.

Many revolutionaries of the West point triumphantly to the fact that Bolshevism is still in power, and apparently, even at the time when these lines are being written (May, 1919), is still outwardly intact; yet the critics of Bolshevism at the very begin- ning of its rule prophesied a speedy collapse. This collapse would have actually taken place long ago, if the Bolsheviks had been true to their programme. They have merely kept themselves going by discarding one after another some part of their programme, so that finally they have achieved the very contrary to that which they set out to obtain. For instance, in order to come into power they threw overboard all their democratic principles. In order to keep them- selves in power they have had to let their Socialist principles go the way of the democratic. They have maintained themselves as individuals; but they have sacrificed their principles, and have proved themselves to be thoroughgoing opportunists.

Bolshevism has, up to the present, triumphed in Russia, but Socialism has already suffered a defeat. We have only to look at the form of society which has developed under the Bolshevik regime, and which was bound so to develop, as soon as the Bolshevik method was applied.

Let us now briefly recapitulate what has been the development. We find in present-day Bolshevik Russia a peasantry established on the basis of unlimited private property and of fullest possibility for production. These peasants live their own lives, without any organic association with town industries. Since these industries cannot produce any surplus goods for the uncultivated land, the voluntary and perfectly legal transport of agricultural products into the towns becomes more and more handicapped. In compensation for this, recourse has been made to requisition, to plundering without payment, on the one hand; and on the other, to illegal smuggling, which succeeds in depleting the towns of the last remnants of industrial products, which have been accumulating for some time past.

After the destruction of the large estates Bolshevism had nothing more to offer the peasants. Indeed, the peasants' love for the Bolshevik was soon changed to hatred for the town workers, who did not work and who could not deliver goods for agricultural purposes; to hatred also against the ruling powers, who sent soldiers into the villages in order to commandeer the commodities; to contempt, moreover, for the town profiteers and smugglers, who seek to foist on the peasants, by all sorts of deceptive means of exchange, their surplus stocks of every kind.

Besides this purely bourgeois state of affairs in the country, there has arisen in the towns a form of society which insists on being socialistic; only it

endeavoured to abolish class differences. It began
by humiliating and destroying the upper classes, and
hence it really threatens to end in a new kind of class-
society. It comprises in fact *three classes*. The
lowest consists of the former bourgeois, capitalists, the
small middle class, and the so-called intellectuals, in
so far as they show any opposition. Deprived of all
political rights, and robbed of all means of subsistence,
they are from time to time forced to do compulsory
labour of the most objectionable kind, for which in
return they receive rations in food, which barely represent the most wretched form of hunger rations, or,
more truly said, starvation rations. The infernal
state of such slavery can only be compared with the
most horrible excesses that capitalism has ever
shown. The creation of this state of affairs is the
original and most characteristic act of the Bolsheviks.
It represents their first step towards the emancipation
of the human race.

Above this lowest class there stands the middle class,
representing the paid workers. This class has political
privileges. It alone, according to the actual words
of the constitution, has a right to vote in the town;
it has, moreover, complete freedom in regard to the
Press, and the right of forming its members into
associated bodies. The members of this class are
allowed to choose their own occupations, and are
sufficiently well paid for the work which they themselves choose. Or rather such was the case; for it soon
became more and more obvious that, as a result
of the low level of the great mass of the workers in
Russia, industry threatened more and more, in consequence of these arrangements, to cease functioning
altogether. In order to save industry, therefore, a
new class of officials had to be formed and put in
authority over the workers. This new class gradually
appropriated to itself all actual and virtual control, and
transformed the freedom of the workers into a mere

illusory freedom. Naturally all this did not happen
without opposition on the part of the workers themselves; and this opposition became all the stronger,
since, in consequence of the general decay, both in
industry as well as in the means of transport and on
account of the increasing isolation of the open land
from the towns, the food problem became more and
more hopeless, even for the workmen, in spite of their
increased wages. So enthusiasm for the Bolsheviks
disappeared from one set of workers after the other.
But the opposition that these latter could offer remained unorganised, dissipated, and could form no com-
pact phalanx in opposition to the more highly organised
bureaucracy. They could not compete with them.

Out of the absolute authority of the Workmen's
Council there developed the absolute authority of a
new class of governors, which was formed, in part, of
representatives who were formerly in the Workmen's
Council; in part of men who were appointed by them;
and also in part of members of a new form of bureaucracy, which was thrust upon them. This new class
of governors was formed under the leadership of the
old Communist idealists and fighters.

The absolutism of the old bureaucracy has come again
to life in a new but, as we have seen, by no means
improved form; and also alongside of this absolutism
are being formed the seeds of a new capitalism, which
is responsible for direct criminal practices, and which
in reality stands on a much lower level than the
industrial capitalism of former days. It is only the
ancient feudal land estate which exists no more.
For its abolition conditions in Russia were ripe.
But they were not ripe for the abolition of
capitalism. This latter system is now undergoing
resuscitation, nevertheless in forms which, for the
proletariat, are more oppressing and more harmful
than those of yore. Private capitalism has now taken
on, in place of the higher industrial forms, the most

wretched and corrupt form of smuggling, of profiteering, and of money speculation. Industrial capitalism, from being a private system, has now become a State capitalism. Formerly the bureaucrats of the State and those of private capital were often very critical, if not directly hostile, towards one another. In consequence the working-man found advantage sometimes with the one, and sometimes with the other. To-day, however, both State and capitalist bureaucracy have merged into one system. That is the final result of the great Socialist upheaval, which the Bolsheviks have introduced. It represents the most oppressive of all forms of despotism that Russia has ever had. The substitution of democracy by the arbitrary rule of the Workmen's Council, which was to serve for the "expropriation of the expropriators," has now given place to the arbitrary rule of a new form of bureaucracy. Thus it has been made possible for this latter to render democracy for the workmen a complete dead letter; since the working-class community has, at the same time, been driven into greater economic dependence than it ever had to endure before.

Moreover, this loss of liberty is not compensated for by increase of prosperity. Certainly the new economic dictatorship functions in a better way than the economic anarchy, which preceded this dictatorship, and which would have led to a sudden end. This end has been merely delayed by the dictatorship; for, economically considered, this new bureaucracy is incapable of functioning.

How very unsatisfactory the functioning of the new organisation has been is proved, among other things, by the following outcry of the Commissioner for Transport, M. Krassin, which he published recently in the "Pravda" (Truth). His manifesto ran as follows:

(1) The existing system of railway administration in combination with the other objective difficulties created

by the Five Years' War, has brought the transport service to complete ruin, which threatens to bring about an absolute cessation of all transport whatsoever.

(2) Its collapse is not attributable merely to faulty methods of administration and forms of organisation, and not merely to the diminished capacity of the personnel, but rather to frequent changes in forms of administration and organisation.

(3) The task which lies before us consists in restoring the transport system to such an extent that at least the needs and requirements of the hunger-rations and of industry may be satisfied. This task can be faced only by the most heroic combination and application of all the strength the railway system can muster.

(4) This work must be undertaken immediately and not a single hour must be delayed; otherwise we are threatened with the destruction of all that has been achieved by the Revolution.

(5) In place of collective administration, which in reality has been wholly irresponsible, the principles of personal administration and of an increased sense of responsibility must be established. Everybody from the office boy to the member of the Governing Board must carry out, exactly and without any deviation, all his full orders. All reforms must be stopped, and, wherever it is possible, the old appointments should be maintained; and the old technical apparatus, both at the centre and in all its ramifications, must be restored and upheld.

(6) The introduction of piece-work is essential.

Of all the Soviet Government officials, Krassin has shown most talent for organisation in a scientific and educated manner, born of experience. The railway workers form, as it were, the élite of the Russian working-class. Already under Tsarist regime it had developed into a good organisation, which always showed great intelligence. Yet in spite of all this, such are the conditions at the present day!

This manifesto shows clearly enough that the consequences of the war are not alone responsible for this necessitous condition, as has often been maintained. These consequences of the war have merely aggravated the stress. It is the immaturity of the existing relations which threatens to destroy all that has been achieved by the Revolution. In order to save the Revolution it seems to be absolutely imperative to discard the reforms, to restore the old positions, and to replace the old apparatus—in other words, to nullify the Revolution of the system, in order to save the men of the Revolution. Naturally enough this decree will succeed in changing the men who are to carry it out as little as any other decrees have succeeded in the past.

Like the old capitalism, this new "communism" has itself produced its own "gravediggers." But the old capitalism did not merely produce these gravediggers; it provided these latter with strength and productive energy to infuse fresh life into what was already moribund.

Communism, under present conditions in Russia, can only do harm to the productive forces that it finds in existence. Its " gravediggers " will not be able to develop some higher form of life, but they will be forced to begin all over again with barbarian forms of life which are coming into existence. Even provisionally such a kind of regime could only continue by having some powerful means of violence to support it, such as a blindly obedient and disciplined army. Such the Bolsheviks have created, and even in this determination their principles had to suffer defeat, in order that they themselves might be saved. They started off with the intention of destroying ready-made State machinery, with all its military and bureaucratic apparatus. After they have settled this, however, they find themselves compelled, in the interests of self-preservation, to erect anew the self-same apparatus. They came into power as pioneers of the dissolution of the army by means of Soldiers' Councils, which were to appoint their own officers at will, and which should obey those whom it pleased them to obey. The Soldiers' Councils, alongside of the Workmen's Councils, formed the Alpha and Omega of Bolshevik policy. By this method they were to become possessed of all power. But after this was done things turned out very differently. As soon as the Bolsheviks met with open opposition they needed an army to fight— one which would be obedient to every command; not an army which was dissolving, or in which the battalions decided on operations according to their own liking. At the beginning, enthusiasm seemed successfully to compensate for sheer blind obedience; but what was to be done when the enthusiasm of the workers began to dwindle, when volunteers became rarer and rarer, and when single divisions of troops began to get out of hand? In industry a democratic system of management and control requires a certain mature development of material, as well as spiritual, conditions. Democracy by its very essence must be excluded from an army that is to be developed up to perfect fighting strength. The war was always the grave of democracy; even civil war, if it went on for any length of time. The Bolsheviks of necessity were responsible for civil war and, as a result also of necessity, for the abolition of the Soldiers' Councils. The Bolshevik dictatorship has reduced these Workmen's Councils to mere shadows, by opposing all sorts of difficulties to the new elections, and by excluding every possible form of opposition. But it has taken from these Soldiers' Councils all their most important functions, and even their right of election of their own officers. As in former days these latter are now appointed by the Government; and since the volunteers are not sufficient, they have had recourse to compulsory recruiting, as in the times before Bolshevism existed. This forms another object of conflict between the population and the Government. Numerous peasant revolts have their origin in this, and it also makes imperative an increase in the army. Desertions in whole numbers belong to the order of the day, and they are punished by mass executions.

The *Humanité* of May 29th, 1919, published a very friendly account of Bolshevism, based on the observations of an eye-witness who had been in Russia. The article under the title of " Les Principes Communistes et leur Application " closed with the following words : " The Red Army is the work of the Entente. The Bolshevik regime has repeatedly proclaimed its anti-militarism. The peace-loving people has as much horror of war to-day as it had yesterday, and at all times in the past. It is making very strong opposition to recruiting—in the Red Army there are as many cases of desertion as there were formerly in the Tsarist Army. It often happens that a regiment does not accomplish what has been prescribed for it, because all the men concerned have fled."

This behaviour on the part of the Red Army is a curious and unusual means of showing its enthusiasm for Bolshevik principles. Even if we merely confined ourselves to facts, without giving them an apologetic foundation, it would seem that in military matters the old Tsarist conditions have returned, only in some worse form; for the new form of militarism without doubt is developing far greater energy than the old, in spite of its proclamation of anti-military discipline.

Thus the conditions are repeating themselves which prepared the way, at the time of the great French Revolution, for the transformation of the Republic into a Napoleonic Empire. But it is certain that Lenin is not destined to end as a Russian Napoleon. The Corsican Bonaparte won his way to the hearts of the French people, because he led the banners of France triumphant throughout the whole of Europe. This satisfied some people that it was the principles of the

Revolution which were conquering Europe. Others, perhaps, were still more satisfied, because the armies of France were plundering the whole of Europe, and their booty was enriching France. But Russia is at present on the defensive. The same difficulties of transport, which would check an army of invasion, prevent Russia from allowing its own army to press triumphantly beyond its own borders. Lenin also would very much like to carry the banners of his Revolution triumphantly throughout Europe, but there is no prospect of that. The revolutionary militarism of the Bolsheviks will not enrich Russia. It can only become a new source of impoverishment. At the present moment Russian industry, in so far as it has been set going again, is working for the army, and not for any productive ends. Russian Communism has, in very fact, become in this respect a sort of "barrack Socialism."

The economic, and with it also the moral failure of Bolshevik methods is inevitable. It can only be veiled over if it should end in a military collapse. No world revolution, no help from without could hinder the economic failure of Bolshevik methods. The task of European Socialism, as against Communism, is quite different, namely, to take care that the moral catastrophe resulting from a particular *method* of Socialism shall not lead to the catastrophe of Socialism in general; and, further, to endeavour to make a sharp distinction between these methods and the Marxist method, and bring this distinction to the knowledge of the masses. Any Radical-Socialist Press must ill understand the interests of social revolution, if it really imagines it serves those interests by proclaiming to the masses the identity of Bolshevism and Socialism, making them believe that the present form of the Soviet Republic, just because it is sailing under the flag of the omnipotence of the working-classes and of Socialism, is in truth the realisation of Socialism itself.

The Terror.

The development we have just sketched did not, of course, arise in accordance with the intentions of the Bolsheviks.   On the contrary, it was really something quite different from what they wanted, and they sought by all means in their power to arrest its develop- ment.   But in the end they had to resort to the same recipe from which the Bolshevik regime from the very beginning had worked, i.e., to the arbitrary force of a few dictators, whom it was impossible to affect by the slightest criticism.   The Regiment of Terror thus became the inevitable result of Communist methods.   It is the desperate attempt to avoid the consequences of its own methods.

Among the phenomena for which Bolshevism has been responsible, Terrorism, which begins with the abolition of every form of freedom of the Press, and ends in a system of wholesale execution, is certainly the most striking and the most repellant of all.   It is that which gave rise to the greatest hatred against the Bolsheviks.   Yet this is really no more than their tragic fate, not their fault—in so far as it is permissible to speak of fault or blame in so enormous an historical upheaval as we are now experiencing.   In any case, at bottom any fault or blame can only be a personal one.   Whoever sets about to discuss a question of culpability must set about to examine the defiance of certain moral laws on the part of individual persons; since the " will " taken in its strictest sense can only be the will of individual persons.   A mass, a class, a nation cannot in reality *will*.   It lacks the necessary faculties for such.   Therefore it cannot sin.   A mass of people or an organisation can act universally.   Nevertheless, the motives of each person actively concerned may be very different. But it is the *motives* which form the determining factor in the question of apportioning culpability.

The motives of the Bolsheviks were certainly of the best. Right from the beginning of their supremacy they showed themselves to be filled with human ideals, which had their origin in the conditions of the proletariat as a class. Their first decree was concerned with the abolition of the death penalty; and yet if we would consider the question of their culpability, we should find that this came to light at the very time when this decree was promulgated, namely, when they decided, in order to gain power, to sacrifice the principles of democracy and of historical materialism, for which they during many long years had fought with unswerving determination. Their culpability comes to light at the time when they, like the Bakunists of Spain in the year 1873, proclaimed the " immediate and complete emancipation of the working-classes," in spite of the backward state of Russia; and with this end in view, since the democracy had not fulfilled their expectations, established their own dictatorship in the name of " The dictatorship of the proletariat." It is here where the culpability can be looked for. From the moment they started on this path they could not avoid terrorism. The idea of a peaceful and yet real dictatorship without violence is an illusion.

The instruments of terrorism were the revolutionary tribunals and the extraordinary commissions, about which we have already spoken. Both have carried on fearful work, quite apart from the so-called military punitive expeditions, the victims of which are incalculable. The number of victims of the extraordinary commissions will never be easy to ascertain. In any case they number their thousands. The lowest estimate puts the number at 6,000; others give the total as double that number, others treble; and over and above these are numberless cases of people who have been immured alive or ill-treated and tortured to death.

Those who defend Bolshevism do so by pointing out that their opponents, the White Guards of the Finns, the Baltic barons, the counter-revolutionary Tsarist generals and admirals have not done any better. But is it a justification of theft to show that others steal? In any case, these others do not go against their own principles, if they deliberately sacrifice human life in order to maintain their power; whereas the Bolsheviks most certainly do. For they thus become unfaithful to the principles of the sanctity of human life, which they themselves openly proclaimed, and by means of which they have themselves become raised to power and justified in their actions. Do we not indeed all equally oppose these barons and generals just because they held human life so cheap and regarded it as a mere means for their own ends? It will be urged, perhaps, that it is the object in view that makes the difference; that the higher object in view should sanctify means, which, in the case of mere seekers after power, become infamous and wicked because of their evil ends. But the end does not justify every means, but only such as are in agreement with that means. A means which is in opposition to the end cannot be sanctified by that end. One should just as little strive to defend one's principles by surrendering them, as to defend one's life by sacrificing what gives to that life content and purpose. Good intentions may excuse those who have recourse to wrong means; but these means nevertheless remain reprehensible, the more so the greater the damage that may be caused by them.

But not even the aim of the Bolsheviks is free from objection. Its immediate endeavour is to preserve the militarist bureaucratic apparatus of power, which it has created; but most certainly this should be done by opposition to the corruption that has made itself manifest within that apparatus.

In the *Pravda* of April 1st, 1919, Prof. Dukelski insisted that Bolshevism and the government institutions should be cleansed of all the rogues and adventurers who had thrown in their lot with Communism, and who were simply exploiting it for their own criminal ends. Whereupon Lenin replied:

" The writer of this letter demands that we should cleanse our Party of the adventurers and rogues—a perfectly justifiable demand which we ourselves have for some time past been making and have carried out. The rogues and adventurers we shoot down, and we shall continue to shoot them down. Yet, in order to carry out more expeditiously and more thoroughly this cleansing process, we need the help of sincere and unbiassed intelligence."

Shooting—that is the Alpha and Omega of Communist government wisdom. Yet does not Lenin himself call upon the " intelligentsia " to help him in the struggle against the rogues and the adventurers? Certainly he does; only he withholds from them the one and only means that can help, namely, *the freedom of the Press*. The control exercised by the Press, in every respect free and unimpeded, alone can keep in check those rogues and adventurers who inevitably fasten on to any Government which is unlimited in its powers and uncontrolled. Indeed, often through the very lack of the freedom of the Press these parasites thrive the more.

Yet the Russian Press is at the present day entirely in the hands of those government institutions in which the rogues and adventurers have found their place. And what guarantee has Lenin, under the present circumstances, that these very rogues and adventurers shall not somehow work their way into the revolutionary tribunals and the extraordinary commissions, and will not cause the sincere and unbiassed " intelligentsia " to be shot down with their aid? It is just the extraordinary commissions instituted to fight corruption which have the most absolute and supreme power. They are entirely free from every form of control, i.e., they work for the most part under conditions that are actually favourable to corruption.

The Revolutionary Tribunal of 1793, even at that time, possessed an unheard-of degree of arbitrary power. The guarantees in favour of the rights of those who were indicted were at a minimum. Nevertheless, the Tribunal at that time did at least function in public, so that a certain control of its activity was possible. But the Extraordinary Commissions of the Soviet Republic deliberate in secret, without any sort of guarantee that the accused shall have their due rights. For it is not absolutely imperative that the accused himself should be heard, let alone his witnesses. A mere denunciation, a mere suspicion suffices to remove him.

This evil took on such enormous dimensions that it had to be abolished. It was therefore determined that these Commissions should no longer proceed to execution without examination and judgment. But despotism is so much of the very essence of dictatorship that it cannot be abolished without abolishing dictatorship as well. Hence this particular decree becomes itself annulled, by reason of an exception which admits summary execution in the case of "obviously counter-revolutionary conspiracy." Thus naturally the door is wide open for every kind of arbitrary execution! If, however, this decision is observed within the proper bounds, it merely succeeds in protecting the robbers and the rogues; but not the sincere and unbiassed "intelligentsia," through whose appearance the Government institutions are to be cleansed. For what is such a cleansing process if it is not a counter-revolution? The slightest expression of discontent is threatened with the same severity as is any form of roguery. And the threat is not rendered abortive by any counter-measure, since it relates to matters in which the sincere communist as well as the rogues have equal interest. For in their criticism of the Soviet regime they both work hand in hand. Hence any modification is out of the question. Thus, quite recently, the "All Russian Extraordinary Commission for Opposing the Counter-Revolution" made the following proclamation:—

"A series of revolts, which have broken out recently, proves that the laurels acquired by Krassnoff, as well as the Socialist revolutionaries of the Left Wing and the Mensheviks of the Left Wing, have not caused them to cease their activity. It is their exclusive aim to undermine our army (Briansk, Samara, and Smolensk), to destroy our industry (Petrograd and Tula), as well as our means of transport and food supply through railway strikes. The 'All Russian Extraordinary Commission' declares herewith that it will make no difference whatever between the White Guards among Krassnoff's troops and the White Guards belonging to the party of the Mensheviks and of the social revolutionaries of the Left Wing. The chastising hand of the Extraordinary Commission will work with equal severity in the one case as well as in the other. The Left Socialist Revolutionaries and the Mensheviks who have been arrested by us will be held as hostages, and their fate will depend entirely upon the attitude of both parties."—President of the All-Russian Extraordinary Commission, F. Jershinski (taken from the *Isvestia* of the All-Russian Central Executive Committee, Number 59, March 1st, 1919).

Hence, because in the army there are signs of dissolution visible, and because discontent is growing among the industrial workers and the railway employees, the leading elements of the non-Bolshevik Socialists are to be arrested, so that they may be summarily shot at the slightest sign of any further proletarian opposition. The quelling of a discontented proletariat—

that is the sublime object with which it is attempted
to sanctify the fatuous means of wholesale executions
in Russia. It cannot possibly turn economic failure
into a success. It can only lead to the possibility
that the fall of Bolshevism will not be accepted by
the masses of Russia in the same way as the fall
of the Second Paris Commune was received by the
whole of the Socialist proletariat at that time; but
rather as the fall of Robespierre of the 9th Thermidor,
1794, was received by the whole of France, namely,
as salvation from some heavy load, and by no means
as a defeat felt with intense pain and sorrow.

The Outlook for the Soviet Republic.

Lenin's government is threatened by another 9th
Thermidor, but it may come about in some other way.
History does not repeat itself. A government that
sets an object in view, which under the circumstances
is unattainable, may go to pieces in two different ways.
It will in the end be overthrown if it stands by its
programme and falls with it. But it can only maintain itself if it makes some corresponding change in
its programme, and finally abandons it altogether.
Whatever happens, one way just as much as the other,
will lead to failure, so far as the thing itself is concerned. For those persons implicated, however, it
makes an enormous difference whether they retain
the State power in their own hands, or whether they
are to be delivered up as fallen idols to the rage and
fury of their enemy.

Robespierre fell on the 9th Thermidor, but not all
the Jacobins shared his fate. By means of clever
adaptation to circumstances many of them rose to a
high position. Napoleon himself originally belonged
to the Terrorists, and indeed was a friend of

Robespierre's brother.   Their sister says later on,
" Bonaparte was a Republican.   I will even go so far
as to say that he was on the side of the 'Mountain.'
His admiration for my elder brother, his friendship
for my younger brother, and perhaps also the sympathy
he showed in my misfortune, were responsible for
my receiving from the Consulate a donation of 3,600
frs." (Quoted by J. H. Rose, "Napoleon I.," 1916,
volume 1, page 50.)

But not only individuals.   Whole parties can so
transform themselves as to extricate themselves from
an untenable position, not only with a whole skin,
but even with enhanced power and respect.   It is
not impossible that the collapse of the communist
experiment in Russia may not equally transform the
Bolsheviks, and save them as a governing party.
They are already on the way.   As thorough-going,
practical politicians, the Bolsheviks have developed the
art of adaptation to circumstances in the course of
their rule to a remarkable degree.   Originally they
were whole-hearted protagonists of a National
Assembly, elected on the strength of a universal and
equal vote.   But they set this aside, as soon as it
stood in their way.   They were thorough-going
opponents of the death penalty, yet they established
a bloody rule.   When democracy was being abandoned
in the State they became fiery upholders of democracy
within the proletariat, but they are repressing this
democracy more and more by means of their personal
dictatorship.   They abolished the piece-work system,
and are now reintroducing it.   At the beginning of
their regime they declared it to be their object to smash
the bureaucratic apparatus, which represented the
means of power of the old State; but they have introduced in its place a new form of bureaucratic rule.
They came into power by dissolving the discipline of
the army, and finally the army itself.   They have
created a new army, severely disciplined.   They

strove to reduce all classes to the same level, instead of which they have called into being a new class distinction.   They have created a class which stands on a lower level than the proletariat, which latter they have raised to a privileged class; and over and above this they have caused still another class to appear, which is in receipt of large incomes and enjoys high privileges.   They hoped in the villages to cripple the peasants who had property, by meting out political rights exclusively to the poorest among the peasantry. Now they have granted these propertied peasants some measure of representation.   They began with a merciless expropriation of capital, and at the present moment are preparing to hand over to American capitalists the mineral treasures of half Russia, in order to gain their assistance, and in every way to come to some terms with foreign capital.   The French war correspondent, Ludovic Naudeau, gave a report recently in the *Temps* of a conversation he had had with Lenin, in which the latter, among other remarks, gave the following account of his friendly attitude towards capital : —

" We are very willing to propose that we should acknowledge and pay the interest on our foreign loans; and since we lack other means of payment, that this should take the form of the delivery of wheat, petroleum, and all kinds of raw material, of which we without doubt have superfluous stocks, as soon as work in Russia can be undertaken to its fullest extent.   We have also decided, on the strength of our contracts, which, of course, must first receive diplomatic sanction, to grant concessions to subjects of the Entente Powers for the exploiting of forests and mines, naturally subject to the condition that the essential basis of government of the Russian Soviet Republic be acknowledged.   We know that English, Japanese, and American capitalists are keenly striving for such concessions."

Interviews are not documents upon which one can swear, but the views of the Soviet Republic, about which we are here speaking, are proved by other responsible reporters on Russia. They give evidence of a strong sense of the actual realities of life; but show that they have already renounced their Communist programme, since its realisation will be delayed for some long time to come, if they are prepared to farm out to foreign capitalists a part of Russia for eighty years. Communism, as a means towards the immediate emancipation of the Russian proletariat, has now collapsed. It is now only a question whether Lenin's government will announce in a veiled manner the bankruptcy of Bolshevik methods, and seek thereby to maintain its position; or whether a counter-revolutionary power will overthrow this government and proclaim its bankruptcy in a very brutal way. We should ourselves prefer the first way, namely, that Bolshevism should once more consciously establish itself on the basis of Marxist evolution, which holds that natural phases of development cannot be precipitated. It would be the least painful, and it would also be the most beneficial way for the International proletariat. But, unfortunately, the course of world-history does not always run according to our wishes. The hereditary sin of Bolshevism has been its suppression of democracy through a form of government, namely, the dictatorship, which has no meaning unless it represents the unlimited and despotic power, either of one single person, or of a small organisation intimately bound together. With a dictatorship it is as with war. This should be borne in mind by those in Germany who are under the influence of the Russian method, and who are now coquetting with the idea of a dictatorship, without thinking it out to its logical conclusion. It is easy to begin a dictatorship as it is to begin war, if one has the State power under control. But when once such steps have been taken, it is as difficult at will to stop the one as the other. One has to choose between two alternatives, either to triumph or to end in catastrophe. Russia has an imperative need of foreign capital. But this help will not be forthcoming to the Soviet Republic, unless it upholds the National Assembly and the freedom of the Press. This is not to imply that the capitalists were ever democratic idealists. Without hesitation they gave millions in support of Tsarism; but they have no strong confidence in regard to the business capacity of the present revolutionary government. They are in doubt as to its constitution, when it suffers no criticism to appear in the Press, and obviously has not the majority of the population behind it. Will the Soviet Government find a way to preserve the freedom of the Press and to convoke a Constituent Assembly? A certain number of Bolsheviks have declared that they fear the one just as little as the other. But why, then, do they not uphold them? Why do they despise a means which, if they use it well, must help towards an enormous increase of their moral strength, and of other people's confidence in them? In the aforementioned preface to Bucharin's "Programme of the Communists" there is written:—

"The conditions which Kautsky and company would impose upon a revolution appear to be that the revolution certainly has the right to dictate its will to the bourgeoisie, but that at the same time it is pledged to grant the bourgeoisie every facility, whether through freedom of the Press or through the Constituent Assembly, to air its complaints. This masterly suggestion of a learned expert, who does not seem to bother whether he has right on his side, but only whether he can lodge his accusation on the particular man for whom he is looking, *might quite well be put into practice, abstractly regarded, without its doing any harm to the Revolution.* But the Revolution consists in being a civil war, and those

classes who have to fight with cannons and machine-
guns readily forego such Homeric form of controversy.
The Revolution never discussed with its enemies. It
destroys them, and the counter-revolution does the
same thing, and both are quite capable of shouldering
the reproof that they have disregarded the orders of
the German Reichstag.''

This justification of slaughter, also in regard to the
counter-revolution, is all the more sublime, when it is
compared with what the author says a few pages before
concerning the revolution :—

" The Socialist Revolution is a long process, which
begins with the dethronement of the capitalist class;
but it can only end with the transformation of the
capitalist system into one for the community of Labour.
*This process will take a generation, at least, in each
country.* This period is exactly the period of the
proletarian dictatorship; the period, that is to say, in
which the proletariat, with one hand, must continue
to crush the capitalist class, while the other hand
alone is free to aid in other Socialistic reconstruction "
(page 18).

That is to say, the revolution is synonymous with
civil war, with a war in which no pardon is given, in
which the one side attempts to crush the other without any lasting effect, since this pleasant process
must continue " for a generation at least." This
devastating civil war, carried on by means of machine-
guns and gas-bombs, which must work more dire
destruction on land than ever happened before in the
Thirty Years' War; which decimates the population,
increases their brutality until it becomes the wildest
barbarism, and which completely stops all sources
of production—this, indeed, is to be the way to the
working out of the higher form of life for which
Socialism stands ! This masterly conception of the
Socialist Revolution is certainly not that of a " learned
expert," but of a professional revolutionary for whom

insurrection is synonymous with revolution, and who really loses his health and life if such revolution assumes the form of democracy, and not that of a civil war. But one thing is certainly correct. There are only two possibilities—either democracy or civil war. Whoever abolishes the one must be prepared for the other. He can only escape from a dictatorship where he has to deal with an absolutely hopeless and apathetic population, which by its very nature represents the lack of human material on which to build the structure of a Socialist society.

As we have only the two alternatives—democracy or civil war—I myself draw the conclusion that wherever Socialism does not appear to be possible on a democratic basis, and where the majority of the population rejects it, its time has not yet fully come. Bolshevism, on the other hand, argues that Socialism can only be introduced by being forced on a majority by a minority, and such can happen only through dictatorship and civil war. The fact alone that Bolshevism feels itself to be in a minority among the people makes it clear why it so obstinately rejects democracy, in spite of its assurance that democracy cannot "harm the revolution." If it thought it had the majority behind it, it would not need to reject democracy, even if it did regard fighting with cannons and machine-guns as the one and only possible form of revolutionary struggle. Moreover, this struggle would be made easier for Bolshevism, as it was for the revolutionary Parisians in 1793, if a revolutionary Convention was behind it all. But such a Convention would not stand behind it. When the Bolsheviks came into power they found themselves at the height of their influence over the workmen, the soldiers, and a large section of the peasants; and yet they themselves at that time did not dare to appeal for a universal election. Instead of dissolving the Constituent Assembly and introducing a new election, they simply smashed

it. Ever since, the opposition against the Bolsheviks
has been increasing from day to day. The growing
nervousness betrayed by its disciples over every
kind of Press which is not official, as well as the
exclusion of Socialist critics from the Soviets, shows
the transition to the Regiment of Terror. In such a
situation, to demolish the dictatorship in order
gradually to return to democracy is scarcely possible.
All such attempts hitherto have quickly come to an
end. The Bolsheviks are prepared, in order to maintain their position, to make all sorts of possible concessions to bureaucracy, to militarism, and to capitalism, whereas any concession to democracy seems to
them to be sheer suicide. And yet that alone offers
any possibility of bringing the civil war to an end,
and of leading Russia again along paths of
economic progress and prosperous development
towards some higher form of existence. Without
democracy Russia will go to pieces; but through
democracy the proletariat must go to pieces. The
final result is quite predictable. It need not be a 9th
Thermidor, but I fear it will not be far removed from
that.

THE OUTLOOK FOR THE WORLD REVOLUTION.

The Bolsheviks themselves seem to have no great
confidence in their ultimate victory. Yet they have
anchored all their hopes on one thing. For if Russia
ceases to be a chosen people of the revolution then
the *World-Revolution* must be the Messiah that
shall redeem the Russian people. But what is this
world-revolution? It may be regarded in two quite
different ways. One may regard it as representing
such a growth of the Socialist idea in the world,
alongside of the strengthening of the proletariat,

accompanied by an increased bitterness of the class-struggle, that Socialism will become a great power, capable of stirring the whole world, and affecting the life of more and more States as it develops. On the other hand, one might understand under this head a revolutionising of the world in the Bolshevik sense, i.e., the conquest of political power by the proletariat in all the great States; otherwise, the Soviet Republic can no longer save the Revolution.   It would mean, further, the establishment everywhere of Soviet Republics, and the depriving of all non-communist elements of their rights.   It would mean the dictatorship of the Communist Party, and, as a consequence, the letting loose of a civil war throughout the whole world for at least a generation to come.

A strenuous propaganda is at work to bring about this result.   To produce a world-revolution, in the Bolshevik sense is beyond their power.   But they might certainly be able, should they succeed, in exerting a very considerable influence on West Europe, and so endanger the world-revolution in the other sense of the word.   For the chief task of the preachers of the world-revolution, in the Russian sense, is the letting loose of a fratricidal war among the proletarian masses of the world.

Being from its very beginning a child of party dissension, and having come to power as the result of its struggle with other Socialist parties of its own country, Bolshevism endeavours to establish itself in Russia by means of a civil war, which makes it into a war between brother and brother; and, as a final means towards its supremacy, it adds the attempt to split up all other Socialist parties which have still remained in unity—so long as they do not prove to have a Bolshevist majority.   Such is the meaning of the Third International.   By this means they hope to introduce the world-revolution.   Yet this is not the consequence of a mere whim or of sheer malice, but proceeds from the very essence of Bolshevism itself, which is incompatible with the higher form of existence, for which pioneer work has already been done in Western Europe.

In Western Europe, democracy is not a thing of yesterday, as is the case with Russia. It has won its way through a series of revolutions, and is the result of a struggle extending over hundreds of years. It has been absorbed by the masses in their very flesh and blood. As a consequence, it is absolutely impossible to deprive all society of all political rights. In France the peasants represent a power which one dare not flout, and which very jealously watches over its own private property. Moreover, the bourgeoisie in France, and still more in England, is a class accustomed to struggle. The proletariat in Russia is certainly weaker than that in West Europe; but infinitely weaker in the Russian Empire is the bourgeoisie itself. There, as everywhere in those countries where a strong military autocracy has been in power, the bourgeoisie is just as much in cowardly fear of the State power, as it is inspired with blind confidence in its protection. Hence the miserable state of present-day Liberalism. The collapse of State power, the failure of the military " wall of protection," the transference of all powers of a State into the hands of the proletariat, so frightened the bourgeoisie, which has never accustomed itself to undertake any energetic political fight, that it absolutely collapsed, and left the ground uncontested in the hands of its opponents.

In West Europe the lower classes, as the result of their class-struggle extending over hundreds of years, have educated not only themselves, but also the upper classes. These latter have gained respect for the proletariat; but they have become, moreover, masters of the art of meeting any attack at the right moment by making concessions, thus avoiding catastrophes. In the Anglo-Saxon countries, however, the bourgeoisie has had, for a long time since, to fend for itself without any strong standing army.   It has learnt, both in relation with the State-power as also with the proletariat, to depend on its own strength alone; hence it does not easily turn tail when any danger is threatened.   And it is these countries that have been victorious in the war.

The war has not crushed and dissolved the armies of these countries as it has those of the Central Powers and Russia.   In East Europe, at the time of the dissolution of the army, it was the soldiers, from whatever class of the population they may have been drawn, who always represented an element of revolt.   But this enormous power, which hastens a revolution, may also have the effect of bringing weak revolutionary factors to power prematurely, thus causing them to be faced with problems which they are not competent to solve.   It is this power which is lacking in the victorious countries.   For there Socialism will only acquire for itself State power, when it is strong enough, within the framework of democracy, to gain the balance over the other parties.   In such countries it has not the slightest cause to abjure democracy; for it is just in such countries that the highest and best strata of the proletariat could never be found ready to accept the substitution of democracy by a dictatorship, which after all simply means the dictatorship of a single person.   It is certain that at the present day in France Bolshevik sympathisers among the Socialists are very strong; but they arose solely in consequence of the very justifiable opposition to all attempts of their own capitalist government to crush Socialist governments abroad.

There are also many who think that Bolshevik methods are suitable for Russia; but they have no intention of recommending the same methods to be applied in France.   Nevertheless, even there the Blanquiste traditions of revolt, and the Proudhonist traditions of anti-parliamentarianism have not quite died out. These two hostile elements have gained fresh life by some strange fusion in syndicalism. They might offer some basis for Bolshevism. But it is quite out of the question that they should ever gain hold of the proletariat of France, or indeed of England and America. Its growth there would only end in its splitting up, just at the time when it would have great and decisive struggles to fight—struggles in which it could only possibly become victorious by showing the utmost cohesion and co-operation. The Bolshevik propaganda for a world-revolution, as we have already said, cannot therefore further the world-revolution, which is already in preparation. The utmost it can do is to endanger it.

Communism, as a result of its diversive tendencies, has already endangered the revolution in Germany. German Social democracy before the war was a strong Socialist party in the country. United on the basis of a common and single aspect of society shared by all its members, it was on the point of embracing the majority of the population, as soon as it had succeeded in winning over the Catholic workers, who followed the banner of the Centrum. If it had possessed the majority, the struggle for democracy, that is to say the struggle for the voting reform in Prussia, would have become a struggle for political power. If this had been gained the party would at once have reaped the finest fruits of its activity, considering the wealth which German capitalism had developed and amassed, and which made it possible to ameliorate rapidly the general condition of the masses. The world-war has made a complete end to this wealth. Peace has now found Germany in the most desperate situation. It precludes any attempt at creating better conditions for the masses, whatever the means of production may be. But this world-war, as a result of the collapse and the dissolution of the army, has also caused

I

social democracy, not through its own strength but through the bankruptcy of its opponents, to come to the fore, at a time when itself has become weakened through the cleavage which the war has brought about. If social democracy wishes to become the dominating party, its immediate reunion has become an imperative necessity. One would have thought that the demands of the present moment would have been carried out all the more expeditiously, since the cause of the cleavage within the Socialist party, namely, the attitude towards the war, has now disappeared.

But, unfortunately, since the rise of the Soviet Republic, a new wedge has been driven through the Socialist ranks of Germany by Bolshevik propaganda, which has demanded that our Party should relinquish the essential claims of democracy, and set up the dictatorship of the workmen's council as a form of State. In order to be under no false impression, the Bolsheviks ceased to call themselves social democrats. They therefore called themselves Communists, apparently in order to ally themselves with the true form of Marxism laid down in the Communist Manifesto. They forgot, however, that Marx and Engels, towards the end of 1847, published the Communist Manifesto, and a few months later issued the *Neue Rheinische Zeitung* as the organ of democracy, so little in their eyes was the antagonism between democracy and communism. The opposition between dictatorship and democracy has created in Germany, alongside of the two Socialist parties which existed before the revolution, yet another, namely, that of the Communists. It has given rise to uncertainty and division in the politics of each of these two parties, and among the Independents has produced strong Bolshevik tendencies. Further, it has resulted in a reaction among a section of the Socialists of the Right against these very tendencies, which, however, overshot the mark, and caused leanings towards the

Bourgeois party, with which the Socialists of the Right, already as the result of the war policy, had a good deal in common.

The revolution of November 9th broke this coalition with the bourgeoisie, and brought about an understanding with the Independents. Unfortunately this was only temporary. In Germany it is just as little possible as in West Europe to introduce a real, permanent, and active form of dictatorship, which should embrace the whole Empire. The population has progressed far too much for this. All attempts of separate and proletarian sections to assume the dictatorship can have only temporary success. They are bound to lead to one result, namely, the increase of the political and economic dissolution of the Empire, and to prepare the way for a counter-revolutionary military dictatorship. But this latter also can never become a permanent and universal power. It is impossible in Germany to continue to govern against the interests of the workers.

The excesses of the Noske Guards in Berlin, the terrible fury in Munich, are no proof of the dictatorial power of the government. They show rather the helplessness of the government in its attitude towards those spirits, which it has conjured up, which are certainly capable of committing with impunity horrible deeds of revenge, but which are nevertheless incapable themselves of guiding the State.

This striving for dictatorship, whether from the Left or the Right, cannot lead to a real dictatorship, but only to anarchy and complete ruin, which will lead us, not to any higher forms of life but to cannibalism, when all production will be at an end, and all food commodities will have been consumed. And even before it can get so far, it may happen that all attempts to introduce a dictatorship will only lead, as the one result of its activity, to an increase of the cruelty and brutality with which political and economic struggles are being

K

fought out, as well as to an increase in the number of victims. This will render any positive construction quite impossible. This is just as true of Noske's regiment as of the Soviet dictatorship.

At the present moment propaganda is being made for a certain form of dictatorship, which is to be only temporary, and which, in any case, is not to have recourse to violence. This is the worst of all possible illusions. In a country in which all classes have already awakened to the importance of political life, no party can exercise a dictatorship without some recourse to despotism. However peaceful their views may be, however great their determination to use the dictatorship merely as a means of acquiring the strength necessary for positive work, it will soon happen, after they have once started their regime, that nothing will remain over of their dictatorial methods but despotism itself.

Democracy alone offers the one means of avoiding despotism, and of coming to some calm and positive construction. But at the present moment democracy has been overpowered theoretically by the Left, and practically by the Right Wing of the Socialist Party. The National Assembly itself is far from being a democracy; for no democracy is possible without the representation of the people by means of a universal and equal vote. The one and only institution at the present moment that might to some extent keep the Empire together can come, not through Workmen's Councils, nor through a dictatorial government, but only through a National Assembly, consisting of representatives from all parts of the Empire. Certainly the present constitution is highly unsatisfactory, but who has elected the majority in it? It is the active population, the very people who are to elect the Workmen's Councils, so soon as these latter have been erected into a system. The votes of the Independent Social Democrats in the constitution form not one-tenth of the National Assembly. The working-classes represent nine-tenths of the whole nation.

The Workmen's Councils present a very different picture from the National Assembly, only so long as they embrace the wage-earners of the great industries. As such, they can become important for progressive policy, and they are indispensable for all attempts at socialisation. But, as such alone, they are incapable of being an adequate substitution for the National Assembly. For the more this system of councils is extended over the whole province of large industry, and the more it embraces the whole of the working population, so much the more must the central council in its constitution approximate to the National Assembly, without investing its majority with that authority which the majority of the National Assembly possesses, as the result of its openly claiming to be the majority of the nation.

Nothing can be more erroneous than the assertion, which has also figured lately in the discussions of the recent Congress of the Third International in Moscow, that parliamentarianism and democracy in their very essentials are bourgeois institutions. They are forms which may be utterly different in content, according to the kind of people they represent. If in any parliament the bourgeois elements are to be in the majority, then parliamentarianism will be bourgeois in character; and if these parties prove to be of no use their parliamentarianism is also useless. But as soon as a Socialist majority appears in Parliament, the whole situation is radically changed. Now it has been said that such a Socialist majority is out of the question, even with the most liberal and complete secret ballot, because the capitalists dominate the Press and buy off the workers. But if the capitalists are really in a position to buy off the workers in this manner, especially after a revolution like the present, they should be just as capable of influencing those

who have the right of voting for these Workmen's
Councils. The further assertion that, for the
Socialists, even by the complete secret ballot, and
even with a majority of wage-earners in the population, it is impossible to gain a majority in any
parliament, on account of the financial power which
the capitalists exercise over the proletariat, is
equivalent to calling the proletariat nothing but a
feeble and cowardly band of illiterates, and simply
announces the bankruptcy of the proletarian cause.
For if the proletariat were of such poor and wretched
constitution, then no institution in the world can help
it, however elaborately it might be decked out to
ensure victory in spite of its moral and intellectual
impotence.

If the German National Assembly of the present day
has a specifically bourgeois character, it is the
Bolshevik propaganda which has contributed not a
little to that. It has caused among the working-classes,
and also among the independents, a certain mistrust
of the National Assembly, and has further impaired the
latter's interests in the elections. And the other working-
class elements, namely, the Catholics, who were on
the point of disassociating themselves from the bourgeois cliques, were likewise weakened, and given over
to bourgeois guidance.

It is quite certain that Germany cannot recover her
health under the *present* National Assembly. The
process of convalescence will not be furthered, but
on the other hand hindered, if the struggle against the
existing Assembly is transformed into a fight against
democracy, against universal suffrage, and against the
constitution of the National Assembly as such. For
in this way a hindrance will be caused, which will
prevent the struggle from concentrating on the one
point where reform can proceed, namely, the election
of a National Assembly, in which the representatives
of the proletariat shall form the majority, and be

prepared to set about as energetically as they can the socialising of the country, in so far as it is possible. They must also be determined unhesitatingly to carry on the democratisation of Germany, which has only just begun. This, and not a dictatorship, must be the programme of any purely Socialist Government that may come into power. In this way it would also gain the allegiance of the Catholic workers, and indeed of all bourgeois circles, if they could see in such a programme the means to help rescue the Republic from the civil war, which has arisen as a result of the dictatorial tendencies among those parties struggling for pre-eminence. If the Communists assert that democracy is none other than the method of *bourgeois* domination, the answer to that would be, that the alternative to democracy, namely, the dictatorship itself, could lead to nothing else but a revolution, and to methods of violence characteristic of byegone days. Democracy, with its universal equal suffrage, does not represent the domination of the bourgeoisie; for the bourgeoisie in its period of revolution did not introduce equal suffrage, but only suffrage according to census, which was introduced into France, England, Belgium and elsewhere. It was only after long and bitter struggle that the proletariat succeeded in acquiring universal and equal suffrage—a perfectly well-known fact, which, however, all Communists and their friends seem to have completely forgotten. Democracy, with its universal equal suffrage, is the method to transform the class-struggle out of a hand-to-hand fight into a battle of intelligence, in which one particular class can triumph only if it is intellectually and morally on a level with its opponent. Democracy is the one and only method through which the higher form of life can be realised, and which Socialism declares is the right of civilised men. Dictatorship leads only to that form of Socialism which has been called Asiatic; but unjustly, for Asia has given birth to a Confucius and a Buddha. It would be more exact to call it *Tartar* Socialism.

Quite apart from the terrible consequences of the world-war, which naturally bear the greater responsibility, it is due in a great measure to the subversive and destructive activity of the Communists, to their dissipation of the strength of the proletariat by fruitless adventures, that the working-classes of Germany have gained little from their own victory, and have not understood how to make democracy an adequate instrument for their own emancipation.

Democracy offers far better prospects for Socialism in West Europe and America. These regions, especially the Anglo-Saxon countries, have issued from the world-war less weakened economically than the others. Every form of progress, and every gain of power on the part of the proletariat, must immediately bring with it an improvement in the conditions of life.

But at the same time the struggle of the proletariat against the bourgeois world must assume more intensive forms than ever it did before the war.

The period of patriotic exuberance, which war and, after it, victory, had given rise to, is rapidly passing. The change has already begun, and will proceed at an increasing rate, when once peace has been signed. For, however great the burdens placed by the Peace Treaty on the conquered, the sacrifices entailed by the victorious peoples will be felt none the less, since everywhere now the chief interest will be turned from external problems to problems of home policy.

The opposition of the proletariat will, in such case, always assume more and more energetic forms, according as its self-consciousness increases. The German, and still more the Russian, Revolution has in this respect acted as an incentive. Whatever one may think of the Bolshevik methods, the fact that a proletarian government in a great State has not only come into power, but been able to maintain itself for nearly two years under the most difficult conditions conceivable, naturally increases the feeling of power among the proletariat of all countries. For the world-revolution therefore, in this respect, the Bolsheviks have rendered an enormous service, far more than they have through their emissaries and propagandists, who have been responsible for more harm to the proletarian cause than for any revolutionary achievement.

The proletariat of the whole world has now been set in motion, and its international pressure will be strong enough to cause all economic progress of the future to develop on Socialist, and no longer on capitalist lines.

In this respect, therefore, the world-war has made this epoch significant; for it has meant the end of capitalist and the beginning of Socialist development. Clearly, we shall not be able to leap at one bound out of a capitalist into a Socialist world. Socialism is not a piece of mechanism, which one can put together on a pre-conceived plan, and which, once it has been set in motion, can go on working in a regular manner. On the contrary, it is in reality a process of social co-operation, which has its own special laws just like any other form of social activity; which however, within these laws can assume the most varied forms, and is also capable of fuller development, the outcome of which it is impossible for us at the present moment to see.

We of the present day have no "ready-made Utopias to introduce by popular decision." What is now happening is the liberating of those elements that mark the beginning of Socialist development. If we care to call that the world-revolution, because this is happening throughout the world, then we are certainly confronted with a world-revolution. It will not proceed on the lines of a dictatorship, nor by means of cannons and guns, nor through the destruction of one's political and social adversaries, but only through democracy and humanity. In this way alone can we hope to arrive at those higher forms of life, the working out of which belongs to the future task of the proletariat.

The National Labour Press, Ltd., Manchester and London. 30842

For Product Safety Concerns and Information please contact our EU
representative GPSR@taylorandfrancis.com
Taylor & Francis Verlag GmbH, Kaufingerstraße 24, 80331 München, Germany